Conversations with a Curator

Understanding and Caring for Aged Textiles and Clothing

ALDA G. KAYE

CONVERSATIONS WITH A CURATOR
UNDERSTANDING AND CARING FOR
AGED TEXTILES AND CLOTHING

Copyright © 2015 Alda G. Kaye.

All photographs in this book are the property of Alda G. Kaye.
Cover Photograph and #18 by Heather Kaye for author.

All rights reserved. No part of this book may be used or reproduced by any means, graphic, electronic, or mechanical, including photocopying, recording, taping or by any information storage retrieval system without the written permission of the author except in the case of brief quotations embodied in critical articles and reviews.

iUniverse books may be ordered through booksellers or by contacting:

iUniverse
1663 Liberty Drive
Bloomington, IN 47403
www.iuniverse.com
1-800-Authors (1-800-288-4677)

Because of the dynamic nature of the Internet, any web addresses or links contained in this book may have changed since publication and may no longer be valid. The views expressed in this work are solely those of the author and do not necessarily reflect the views of the publisher, and the publisher hereby disclaims any responsibility for them.

Any people depicted in stock imagery provided by Thinkstock are models, and such images are being used for illustrative purposes only.
Certain stock imagery © Thinkstock.

ISBN: 978-1-4917-6271-4 (sc)
ISBN: 978-1-4917-6273-8 (hc)
ISBN: 978-1-4917-6272-1 (e)

Library of Congress Control Number: 2015904078

Print information available on the last page.

iUniverse rev. date: 10/15/2015

For my family and others who love and
care for our textile history

Contents

Preface xi
Introduction xv

Chapter 1	Closets—Where many start 1
Chapter 2	Different Times—Who we were 11
Chapter 3	Fashion Snippets—Noticing details 19
Chapter 4	Bits and Pieces—Quilts, coverlets and other flat textiles 29
Chapter 5	All Natural—Fresh from the farm 39
Chapter 6	Summer Heat—Age rediscovered 48
Chapter 7	Oh No!—What did I do? 57
Chapter 8	The Shawl and the Piano—Dealers displaying their goods 66
Chapter 9	Arms and Legs—Lots of things to think about 73
Chapter 10	Lessons to Learn—Walking through a textile and costume collection 86
Chapter 11	Show Biz—Clothing the actor and others 99
Chapter 12	Treasures Found—Saving for the next appearance 107

Summary 115
Postscript 123

List of Photographs

1. Scrimshaw. 7
2. Little girl in photograph with clues that help date it. 15
3. Detail of embroidery, gentleman's coat, late eighteenth
   century. 25
4. Author's sketch of an early quilting frame................................31
5. Detail of appliqued design, hand quilted...................................34
6. Hand-sewn quilt with Masonic insignia, circa 1910................. 35
7. Slater Mill—first cotton-spinning factory in America, 1793.......38
8. Loom for hand weaving, early to mid-nineteenth century............42
9. Handwoven coverlets, late nineteenth century..........................44
10. Early nineteenth-century chair, draped with a paisley shawl....54
11. Casing example for textile display...56
12. Wet cleaning a large, aged textile in handmade container.........64
13. Quilts displayed outdoors, in danger of fading........................70
14. Restored theater costume on exhibit, 2006, Newport, Rhode
    Island. 77
15. Historic holoku on exhibit, 1994, University of Hawaii at
    Manoa, Oahu, Hawaii. 78
16. Hanger cover examples. 80
17. American quilts on exhibit, 1986, University of Rhode Island,
    Kingston, Rhode Island. 94
18. Author in costume, 1997, on movie set................................. 102
19. Four-poster bed, trunk, and quilt, nineteenth century.............111

Preface

When first coming in contact with historic clothing and textiles, of course I couldn't help but be amazed. The thought that this "mirror of the past" was not only visible but also tangible to me at that very moment was exciting. I began wondering, even as a child, how I might have looked in one of those beautiful antique garments, if I had lived such a long time ago.

The years went by, and I attended college, earning a BS degree (University of Rhode Island). And then while working part-time, I continued my education, attending art school and studying interior design (Rhode Island School of Design). Soon after that I got married, and started a family. During that period, I applied for and was awarded a graduate assistantship at the University of Rhode Island and earned an MS degree, majoring in historic textiles. Shortly after that, my new career began. I became the curator of a very large university historic costume and textile collection, and since then, have worked with faculty, students, museums, and other institutions here and abroad for almost thirty years. I have also designed and installed a number of museum exhibitions and storage facilities for institutions in New England, Hawaii, and elsewhere. I was knighted in 2008 (Dame of Honor, Knights of the Orthodox Order of St. John, Russian Grand Priory) for my work at a Newport, Rhode Island, mansion, where I curated a collection of textiles from the medieval and Renaissance periods. I have continued to be involved in research projects, teaching, and other work in the museum field.

It was when I became a university curator, that individuals from outside the university began to phone or come to my office with questions about their own aged textiles, clothing, and related objects. They wanted to gather information on how to take care of them and learn how to use them properly. Even though I left the university and moved on to other positions, the questions have continued.

People are curious. When people own an object of great age that is part of a family history or someone else's that is significant, the thought that what they have might actually have some value can certainly be a strong motivation for them to want to know more about it. They will probably also want information on how to keep it safe for the future. There are many of us who are collectors of sorts, and we take pride in our possessions. Therefore, we want to think carefully when investing in such objects, about what we hope to achieve.

For example, some of us want to save a special garment we wore for a wedding, anniversary, or another occasion. We may want to use it again someday or pass it down to another person or perhaps to a theater group for future use.

Some collectors buy antique textiles and clothing to keep or sell, and they want to do some research on their collections, to learn more about them and whether or not they have value. Others may have purchased a beautiful vintage garment in an antique shop to actually wear, and they realize they need to know more about how to handle it properly.

Antique dealers and other shop owners with attractive, valuable, and interesting, old textile items in stock to sell may find they want some guidance on how to display them safely and more effectively.

Historical societies and small house museums with limited budgets might appreciate additional information on safely displaying, organizing, and storing their collections of historic textiles and related objects.

And so it seems that many of us have reasons for owning or working with particular aged textile items, and we want to protect them in the best way we can. It is always the responsibility of the owners or the ones in charge to decide how they will care for those aged textile treasures, and hopefully with more understanding, each person will make the proper choices.

I have written this book primarily because I want to share my knowledge and ideas and perhaps be of help to others who have questions about caring for vintage fashion, historic textiles, clothing, and other related objects, to understand aged textiles a little better. I have attempted to present the information in a clear fashion and have also added some commonsense observations. It is my wish that my book be helpful, educational, and interesting. You will find that I have introduced each chapter with a relevant personal story. I have done this to help illustrate what I will be discussing and to make it more fun for you to read. I hope that you will find this helpful as we delve into the subject matter. Now, I invite you to follow me and listen to the "conversations" as I share some of my knowledge and experiences.

Introduction

Many people are indeed curious about how to care for aged textile objects. The first question that often comes to mind is, "What is one to do with an interesting textile or an intriguing and maybe wearable relic?" It is true that it can be exciting for someone who has discovered a unique, beautiful, or interesting, old textile item. That is especially so when one really owns such a treasure, whether it be purchased, inherited, or given into one's care. Myriad questions may arise, however, when owners suddenly realize that they now need to have information on how to deal with it. Apprehension might be the result when trying to decide how to handle a new possession properly, and it can become confusing for the owner or other individual in charge.

Some people do not realize they should use special care when handling their old textiles, and they might not bother to ask for help. Others may not think that it is necessary, or perhaps they don't think they have the time to devote to tracking down specific information. There are also those who attempt to obtain assistance or advice from museum professionals and universities dealing with aged textiles, and they discover that help is not readily available.

I believe that if one could only find a way to perhaps just stop for a moment and refrain from handling textiles of some age until one has enough information on proper handling and treatment, there would be a much better chance that the object could be used again in some manner without damage occurring. Having helpful information on hand can certainly be a valuable resource if you have a garment or other textile you want to display, wear, or store properly.

Many items have been accidently destroyed because well-meaning people tried to "improve" their treasures without understanding what they had and why it needed special consideration. People sometimes move too quickly with good intentions and find that they made mistakes in the process, causing a loss in historical and financial value. Some people who have not cared for their objects carefully may even suffer emotionally, especially if it is a family heirloom that is ruined. And a dealer might suffer financially if quality and value of his or her goods is lost or diminished because of improper handling or lack of proper display knowledge. Small museums and historical societies also need relevant information to protect objects they are responsible for.

We would all enjoy our treasures more if we knew we were taking good care of them. It has often been my experience that many people want some commonsense knowledge readily available on how to protect their aged textiles, clothing, and related objects, and guidance is much appreciated. I believe that we really do need to be aware that if there is doubt, that is when we will want to gather more information before proceeding. Throughout the following chapters, I shall discuss this and more.

Collectors and others have asked me countless times to write about all of this. Consequently, this book is intended to serve as a guide for those who want help in understanding more about caring for aged textiles. I have attempted to provide information from my own experiences in the field that may be helpful to others. I like to think of this book as a conversation between the person with questions concerning aged textiles and me.

What I will be talking about are some of what I consider the most important points I have learned and taught in my years working with aged textiles. This book is meant to be for individuals, collectors, antique dealers, small museum staff, historical societies, and others seeking more understanding on how to protect and utilize aged textiles.

I believe that when basically experimenting to try to provide care for an aged textile, without the information that could help one understand how to handle it properly, one is taking a chance that may or may not have good results, and that can be risky. It is my opinion that one should certainly try to acquire some reasonable understanding of any aged textile object that one intends to be involved with before attempting to do anything with it. One might also want to consider including commonsense in the thinking process.

Please note that the information here is based on my knowledge and my experiences. It is not to be a substitute for treatment by a professional when needed. Also, when reading this book, you might be tempted to just select the chapters that appear to answer your questions at first glance, but I suggest that you read the whole book through first for general information, because it may help get you better acquainted with how the book is organized. By doing this, it will give you a little more understanding of the subject matter. Then you might find it easier to decide how it might best suit your own needs. When you read the introductory story for each chapter, you might want to look for clues that I have included that relate to the particular subject matter that will be discussed.

The information in this book is intended to be of help to those wanting some information on the handling, preparing, exhibiting, wearing, and storing of aged textiles and related objects, and it provides some notes on textile and costume history.

Of course if you choose to work with any of what is discussed in this book, remember that any decisions you choose to make in that regard are entirely your own. I certainly do hope you will find that what I have to say is of help to you in gaining a better understanding of aged textiles.

May you have a good experience working with what you have inherited, purchased, or are in charge of. At the same time, also try to remember that when you own or are responsible for a piece of history, it is a candidate for special care, and it really deserves to be protected. It is my sincere wish that you will be as amazed and inspired as I was, when gazing upon my first discovery, and that you fully enjoy the experience!

Chapter 1

Closets

When I was about six or seven years old, I was sitting on my grandmother's bed, watching her while she was preparing to change from her cotton housedress and apron into a more formal outfit. We were going to go shopping downtown with my mother and my little sister shortly, and I was looking forward to a wonderful afternoon! The sun was shining through the dainty lace curtains hanging in my grandmother's bedroom windows, and as the light filtered through them, I noticed how it gave a soft glow to the pink and blue flowers on her bedroom wallpaper.

I loved visiting my grandparents and found them always glad to see me too. I enjoyed being with them, asking questions and learning new things. It was my grandfather who especially liked to talk about the "olden days," and he would tell me lots of interesting stories about what it was like when he was young.

Today, I was chatting with my grandmother. She had just finished selecting the dress she was going to wear to go shopping and was hanging it on a hook on her closet door. The closet door was open, and I could see almost everything in it from where I was sitting on her bed. That was when I noticed a pair of shoes in the closet that I had never seen before. They seemed quite unusual, and I wondered why they looked so different.

"Grammie, what kind of shoes are those?" I asked, pointing at them.

She turned around, reached into her closet, picked up the shoes, and brought them over to the bed to show them to me. She said that they were an old pair of high-button shoes and that she didn't wear them anymore. I asked her why she didn't, and she said, "Because they are way too old-fashioned and too small anyway, and would be very uncomfortable." I looked at the shoes even more carefully now. They were of black leather with little heels and had many small, black buttons on the front. I had never seen shoes with so many buttons before! They were very interesting indeed.

While I was thinking intently about buttons, evidently my grandmother was noticing how much attention I was giving to the shoes, because she walked to her dresser and picked up a strange-looking instrument from a small crystal vase. She brought it over to show it to me and said that it was a tool called a "buttonhook." Then she showed me how it helped to button the shoes for her. I was fascinated! My grandmother also told me the shoes were made of very nice kid leather and that when she was young and they were in style, they made her feet look tiny, and she used to love to wear them. She playfully winked at me and said, "Those shoes bring back some good memories from long ago."

I continued to watch my grandmother, and we kept right on chatting while she changed from the dress she was wearing into a more formal-looking one. That was when I happened to notice something else that made me curious. She was wearing an interesting-looking undergarment. It had lots of laces pulled very tight and sort of reminded me of the shoes we had just talked about, and so I felt I had to ask her about it. I was told that it was called a corset, and she said that when she was young, she had "quite a figure wearing it." Then she said, "In those days, we all wore them because having a tiny waist, like tiny feet, was also very desirable, and a corset was needed to help keep one's figure in shape for the fashions worn then." My grandmother also told me that through the years she continued to wear one. "Now," she said with a sigh, "I can't manage without it because of wearing one for so long." She zipped up her dress and then walked over to her dresser to comb her hair.

I happily observed my stylishly dressed grandmother who was now all finished changing clothes and watched her as she put on her jewelry. When that was all done, she turned toward me with a smile, took my hands, and told me we were now ready to go shopping! She helped me down off the bed, and as we walked out of her bedroom, I looked back at her closet with delight, silently wondering to myself what other kinds of treasures might be lurking inside. I think that afternoon was the very beginning of my interest in old-fashioned clothing.

Now, as we begin our journey together, I would like to start by discussing some of the material in my preceding story. I titled it "Closets" because many searches for answers regarding what to do with aged textiles, clothing, and other related objects begin with what is discovered in closets.

If you were to look into your closet, you might realize that you are somewhat sentimental about a particular garment or other item there. Perhaps it is one you wore when you were younger for a special occasion, and you still treasure the memories attached to it. If so, then you would understand how others might feel the same way. Of course, some might have worn it in a different time period many years ago, but like you, they thought it was important to keep the particular item. Perhaps they were hoping to use it again in some way in the future, but that future use never materialized, and so the object remained sequestered for a long time. Eventually, it was found by someone else and then made its way to another person, the trash, a secondhand shop, an antique shop, a theater, or museum collection. Where it went next would determine its future.

Strange as it may seem, I have spoken with people who found textile objects and even shoes in quite unusual places, including between walls and behind fireplaces, when they were renovating very old houses. I was told that some very interesting textiles were found in the ground beneath an old, deserted outhouse that was on a farm. It was not uncommon in the past for people to have an area on their property where things no longer needed were just piled up over the years, to decay in a mound behind the barn. Some of these actions relate to customs and habits long forgotten. However, occasionally some of those long-ago discarded items surface, and in the process, they prove to be historically important and quite valuable.

But let us not underestimate the closet. A closet containing aged clothing and other such items can be quite exciting, especially when you find something that you think is very interesting. Perhaps the object you find is a dress that was in fashion many years ago. Now try to imagine how the woman who originally wore it felt when she was wearing it. Was it tight? Was the fabric rather heavy with that long skirt, making the dress hard to walk in? Think about the shape. Perhaps it was worn with a corset, and the lady also wore a shawl over her low-cut neckline to stay warm. Look at the waistline and see how very small it is and note that the whole bodice is rather stiff when you handle it. What is making it feel that way? Are there stays or other kinds of support sewn within the bodice? Notice the trimmings on the dress. Are there buttons, ribbons, or lace accents perhaps? Are they rather plain looking or very elaborate? You might find it is intriguing thinking about what time in history that garment may have been worn and for what kind of occasion. You may also wonder if you could find out who the original owner was.

By asking questions and searching for the answers, one begins the research process. Although we will not get into great detail here concerning dating objects, we will discuss it briefly. When discovering old clothing and other textile objects that look rather strange or different to us (because they are from a time we are not familiar with), often research needs to be done. Dating objects is important, and to an inexperienced eye, it may seem difficult, but of course you can seek help online and from other sources. The more one learns about the different periods in fashion and textile history, the more one will understand.

We may indeed find that there are clues presenting us with some of the information, if we just begin to look for them. Let's just think for a moment about my grandmother in the story and her high-button shoes that I admired as a small child. Knowing the birthdate of my grandmother might help tell us when she would have most likely worn those shoes. Finding dated photos of her wearing them could certainly provide us with some information. But, unfortunately, not everyone writes down dates on the backs of photos.

One would want to do research on the time periods when high-button shoes were in fashion and compare the different styles of such shoes. High-button shoes were worn in several time periods with subtle differences in styles. They not only were an example of a style of the time but had a practical side as well that related to the clothing and activities of the period. Studying the history of such types of shoes may help one find the particular time when the use of certain types of buttons, shoelaces, toe and heel shapes, and so on were in fashion.

One way to identify period clothing is to look for characteristic construction and silhouette. Remember that we also discussed restrictive clothing items in the story about my grandmother. Corseting has a long history of note and was popular in many periods, helping to keep the person in the shape needed to fit the outer garment. There were many different types of constriction used, such as cording, ties, pieces of wood, and bone of various shapes. Some corsets were like the one my grandmother wore when she was young, but there were lots of other types worn in many different periods long before.

Men are not to be forgotten, for they wore various restrictive clothing items over the years as well. An example would be heavily starched collars and cuffs, which were actually very stiff and almost razor sharp, worn with dress shirts in different periods.

Another type of corset for women, worn in our early years in America, had a different kind of constrictive device in it called a busk. I had the opportunity to study several that were worn in the late seventeenth and early eighteenth centuries. One busk was five or six inches long and was inserted into a hand-sewn placket located in the center front of a cloth corset. (It had the shape of a large tongue depressor.) The back of the corset was laced, but it was evident that the busk in front was placed there to help maintain a certain posture, which was flat and stiff, made for the fashions of a particular period. I have seen other busks as well in different shapes and sizes, but they are all a rather rare find.

Not all busks were made of wood. Some were actually made of whalebone and had scrimshaw designs of sailing ships and other nautical scenes. These denote a time in our history in America when whaling was popular. They were often done by seamen aboard whaling vessels to be given to a special person as a gift. Some have inscriptions with names of ships or sweethearts, or maybe a poem that might help to date them.

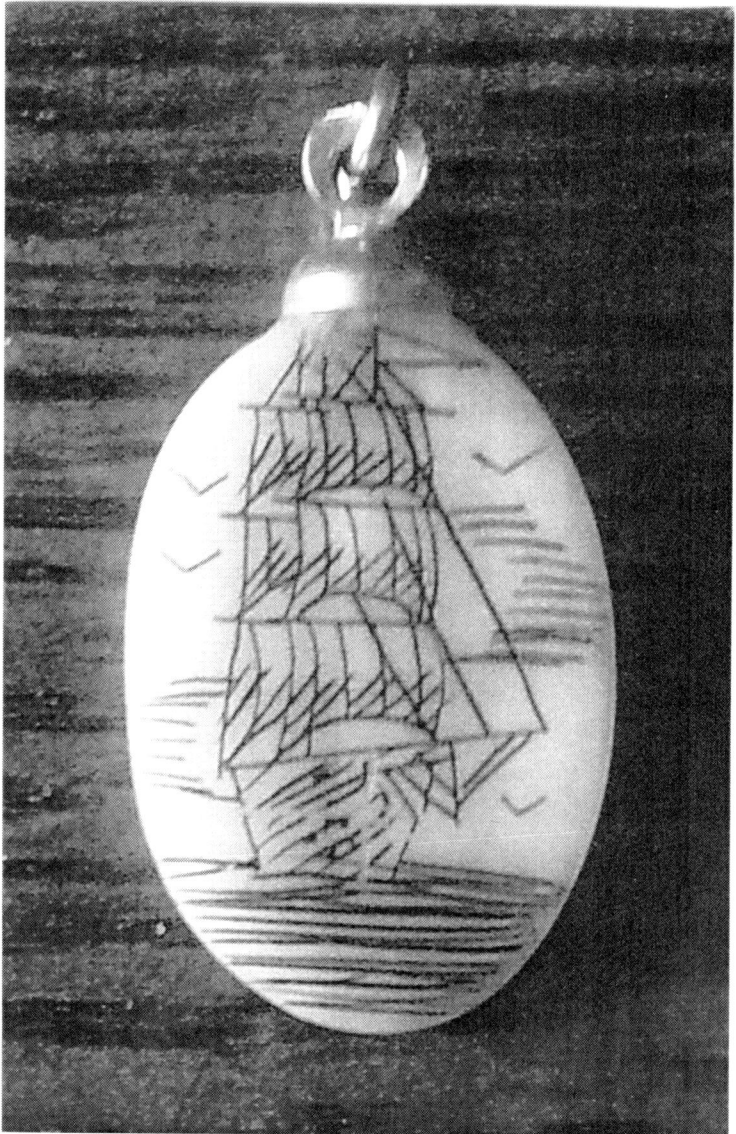

Figure 1. Scrimshaw.

Again, research is important if we want answers to our questions, and there are many places where one can begin. Individuals and small institutions store artifacts of all kinds in closets and attics of old houses. Historic house museums, historical societies, and some shops may even possess items they are totally unaware of owning—items that were stored away by others long ago and that have remained out of sight for many years. Staff might have changed numerous times, and records showing where such artifacts were put away could have been lost, misfiled, or destroyed. Some of these may be historically valuable items that need special care and are just waiting to be rescued.

A while ago, a well-known historical society received a grant to hire me to organize their textile collections that were in the attic of one of the society's oldest buildings, built in the eighteenth century. The director told me that what I would be working with was a collection of textile objects that had been put away many years before. He said that because the main focus of that historic house was the furniture and not textiles, the contents of the attic had been pretty much forgotten about. He had decided it was time for them to be better identified and to receive more proper care. Because of my expertise, I was to examine and document everything in the attic and make sure that the inventory was complete. When I finished that part of the project, I had to design a new storage area for the textiles, clothing, and other objects.

The attic was very dark with few windows in that eighteenth-century building that had been someone's home long ago. The roof had been leaking off and on over the years and patched whenever necessary, and in certain places there were stains that the leaks had left on the interior walls. There were a lot more items in the attic than anyone previously had thought, and because I had been asked to inventory everything there, it was quite time-consuming.

While moving about in the dimly lit attic, I noticed there were many storage containers. I had to carefully empty all the old cabinets and trunks one by one, identify the objects, and make lists of all the contents. While doing that, I came upon a solitary item that was not in a cabinet but actually hanging on a huge iron nail on a wall along one side of the room. It was hanging straight down in a darkened area, and as I looked at it with my flashlight in hand, I noticed it had a few stains, probably evidence of rain that had leaked through the roof at some earlier time. The object looked like a man's garment and was quite long and fairly heavy. It seemed to be constructed of linen-like fabric and was of a neutral color. It appeared to me to be a very early cloak, with a large collar or hood. I examined the cloak carefully with my flashlight and found a rectangular paper tag attached to it. There were a few numbers written on the tag in old-fashioned handwriting or script. I sensed that this object was something valuable and was quite excited with my find. As I studied the cloak a little more, I was convinced that it was from the seventeenth century, and I thought that it had once probably belonged to a man of importance, because of the quality of the fabric and the garment's construction.

I contacted the director and informed him of my discovery. He was unaware of the cloak, and I told him what I thought it was, and we speculated on who might have worn it. The tag said little, and I needed to examine it more closely and try to retrieve information, if any existed, in the society's records. It would take time, and so the cloak and tag were put aside temporarily for further study. Eventually the cloak was fully documented, and we found it to be quite a treasure, for it was a good example of the type of clothing worn by those who were settlers of note in early New England.

These discoveries still happen occasionally but not as often as some of us would like, partly because old historic houses are often changing hands. Not everyone knows what might be important when they find aged items in an attic or other places in old buildings, and they may just throw them away. Hopefully they don't and realize that they may have something of value and donate them, or perhaps loan them to their local historical society or other such facility, but one never can be sure.

I do believe that there are still treasures to be found. Of course when any old building, historical society, or house museum has an attic, cellar, or other buildings close by, there very well may be old artifacts, including textiles, somewhere on the property. This is true particularly when no one has moved in a long while or searched the attic. And if objects are found that have been sequestered for long periods, and no one there is particularly knowledgeable about what they are, they may certainly be in danger of being destroyed unknowingly. It is important to remember that a valuable piece of history may be packed away somewhere in a closet, in a trunk, or even hanging on a nail in an attic, just waiting to be rediscovered. Be aware and you may find a treasure!

Chapter 2

Different Times

During our lifetimes, we have numerous experiences leaving us with unforgettable memories and often some surprises as well. As I sift through my memories, I remember one that happened years ago when my great aunt passed away. I had been invited by family to go to her house and choose a few remembrances. She had a very large, beautiful old house with wonderful antiques. Other relatives had recently claimed some of the furnishings, but there were still some treasures remaining.

I quietly walked through the house, thinking about the times I visited my aunt when she was alive and enjoyed her homemade butter cake, hot tea, and conversations. I also remembered listening to the old clock on the table that chimed quite often, and how much I admired the colorful needlepoint cushions she had created that decorated her front parlor. I also thought about how happy she seemed to be whenever I visited her with my little daughter. She would welcome us with a big smile and then walk slowly with cane in hand into her kitchen to get her tiny visitor some milk and a cookie or two. I quietly mused about how sweet and dear my aunt was. Now I had only the memories.

But it was time to come back to the present moment. I had a quest, which was to find my special remembrance. After looking around a little bit more, I went upstairs to the second floor. I spent some time there and then climbed the stairs to the third floor, for it was a big house with lots of rooms. I browsed some more for a while and then decided to climb the smaller stairs to the attic. I always liked attics, imagining them intriguing and filled with secrets.

I opened the door to the attic, peering inside to see what was stored there, and it was then that I happened upon my treasure! It looked like it was a very old chest or maybe a trunk over by the attic window. The sun was shining brightly through the window right on it, and I could see it clearly. It was large and rectangular in shape and of a tan color, with a covering that looked like tightly woven bamboo. There were pretty metal handles on either side of it, and I thought it was quite attractive. This was definitely my treasure. I was very excited to have found it and could hardly wait to see what was inside, imagining all kinds of things, but I really didn't know what to expect. I just knew it was what I wanted.

Kneeling down in front of my discovery, I happily decided I would open it right away and look to see what it contained. When I opened it, I saw a large interior filled with many garments. There were several small, removable trays on top that held some objects as well. Everything appeared to be wrapped or layered in clean, white sheeting, and I noticed that the chest was air tight, which helped to protect everything inside. I thought it best to wait until I could get it home before disturbing the contents, and a few days later when it was in my home, I carefully delved into it.

There were many beautifully handmade petticoats of white cotton with hand-embroidered eyelet, and some of lightweight silk in pastel shades of green and pink, all hand sewn. I also found several long skirts of heavier silk with ruffled hems. There were beautiful lace collars and a few little jackets trimmed with velvet ribbons, and pretty bodices that seemed to match the very long skirts. I also came across two bathing suits. One was probably my aunt's and was made of an attractive blue wool fabric with white wool trim and a belt of white canvas with a metal buckle. The other had to have belonged to my uncle, for it was very large, like him. It was also made from wool and was all black. I eventually donated these bathing suits to the collection at the University of Rhode Island (URI), just a few donations of many I made to that collection over the years.

Most everything in the chest appeared to be dated from approximately 1880 to 1918. Among the smaller objects I found in the chest were about a half-dozen beautifully hand-sewn baby dresses, still in pristine condition. I was puzzled to see the beautiful baby clothing, however, because I knew that my aunt and uncle had never had children. I wondered about that. Later on, I asked my mother about the dresses, and she told me that sadly their baby had been stillborn. My aunt must have made the baby clothes while she and my uncle were waiting for their baby to arrive. It had to have been very hard for them to lose their child, and I could imagine my aunt silently packing the little garments away in that chest many years ago, perhaps hoping there would be another chance to use them some day. But that time never came.

Take note that there are often silent stories wrapped up in textiles and other aged objects that we find. I thought back to all the times my aunt loved spoiling my little girl and remembered how much she enjoyed it when I brought her along with me on a visit. Now I understood. The chest had much to tell me about a time long ago. I treasure the memories, and much of what was in it remains part of my costume collection today.

And so we begin. Many of us have inherited treasures from the past or sought them out, looking for something unique and special. Owning a piece of history can be exciting. Those who have sorted through the racks of old clothes in antique shops and other places where such items are for sale are often very curious. They want to know more and have many questions, such as: How old are they? How were they worn originally? How much are they worth? Are they wearable or usable in some way now? What is the best way to care for them? And so on.

You might purchase an old garment or other antique item, such as a nineteenth-century quilt, or open an old trunk and find that you have inherited some antique treasures. An object in that trunk might be a precious piece of your family history or someone else's. Perhaps it will become a significant addition to your home décor, or be used in a special function or ceremony, or become a donation of significance to a museum or historical society, or even be put up for sale in a shop.

Because our grandparents and recent ancestors may have packed favorite textiles away, it is possible that there are many wonderful treasures out there for us to find. We might even discover something from our more recent past. For example, perhaps you might find an elegant wedding gown that belonged to a favorite aunt, or a small child's outfit that you saw before in a photograph in the family album.

Figure 2. Little girl in photograph with clues that help date it.

All are just waiting to be rediscovered. We have lost track of so much of our past with our busy lives, but what an exciting adventure it can be to uncover it again in such an interesting way. The ranges of styles and fabrics might make us want to have a conversation about our ancestors with an elderly family member, find a helpful book at a library, visit a museum, or search online in order that we may learn more. It certainly can be lots of fun if one has the time.

Many beautiful gowns and other garments, as well as men's and women's wedding clothes, were packed away years ago with extra care to be carefully sequestered and lovingly remembered. Be aware that if you are lucky enough to uncover one of these special treasures, it might also contain a handwritten letter or label, with names and dates and other information nestled or sewn carefully within or on the item. I have often discovered a letter or label written in black ink on a piece of paper or fabric sewn within a wedding gown or jacket from earlier periods. It was most likely placed there by the original owner or perhaps by someone close to that person. I have also found names and dates written in ink or embroidered on some old quilts. All are meant to provide information and identification, and they can be welcome pieces of history for the person discovering them.

When you find such items, you will want to examine each piece very carefully because information found in a chest or trunk or with any accessories, such as purses or shoes, for example, may contain clues to help date and identify the previous owners. Sometimes old saved letters may have information that will give you a window into the past and astound you. Interestingly enough, I have found that garments were listed in wills in earlier times, along with home furnishings and other objects, because they were of great value to families. Remember that if you find letters and such, handle them very carefully, for they may be fragile. Because they are probably much older than they sometimes appear to be, they may not be as sturdy as you think they are.

Whenever I handle any aged textile, I always remember to be sure to wash my hands before I pick it up, and I often wear clean, white gloves as well. When handling any textiles of some age, it is important to have clean hands because perspiration, hand lotions, perfume, and so forth, may leave a residue on an old textile fabric that could react over time. Also, rings and other jewelry are removed because they might catch on an object. If I am handling a lot of items, I will wash my hands often and change gloves when need be. Inexpensive, thin, cotton gloves purchased in drugstores or ordered from conservation supply companies are very useful for handling aged objects.

Now, I want you to think about what one can do with what seems to be a wearable relic. What do we do when we discover old clothing and other textiles that have been packed away to be saved for a special reason? What do we see? If the objects look to be hand sewn and look really old, be aware. Look closely. You may see interesting and very beautiful details you have never seen before. Hand-stitched artistry, as it were, displaying corded seams, padded hems and lapels, and other details of earlier construction, all illustrating the skill and time that went into constructing these garments.

Perhaps one will see riches in abundance and luxuries to be treasured! If what is uncovered is very old, maybe from our early forefathers' time, there could be dainty floral prints, sheer gauzes, smooth satins, rich silk velvets, thick woolens, crisp silks and linens, elaborate trimmings, handmade laces, interesting ribbons, and fascinating buttons that adorned many of those before us. All are wonderful remnants from time gone by. If a garment is a designer original, it may also be hand sewn and have fine details. If you are lucky enough to find a designer label, you may want to do some research on the designer, and your treasure may take on a whole new meaning.

Because we live in a different time, we may find that we don't always understand what it is we are looking at and what clues might be presenting themselves. We have to look more closely to understand what we need to pay attention to. Not everything is easy to find. One must be observant and do research. Also, if you find that you have access to any museum professionals, one may be able to help steer you in the right direction to gather some additional information.

I find that old motion pictures surviving from the twentieth century, produced in and for the actual time they were being filmed, are good sources for viewing fashions of that period. While watching the credits at the end of a film, one may see information that includes the date of the film along with the names of costume designers. I find this valuable because the clothing is authentic to the period and gives a true representation that can be referred to when one is attempting to identify clothing today from that period.

When working with period films set in a particular decade or century, well-known costume designers sometimes make the costumes. These films are usually researched carefully, and watching them can help you become familiar with some of the styles and silhouettes of the particular periods being portrayed. However, when watching some of these films, I have seen mistakes many people probably wouldn't know were mistakes because of my experience working extensively with original historic clothing. These films are okay in most situations, however, because they can be of help when you are starting out and trying to learn some of the basics of different periods. In the next chapter, we shall go into more detail on what to look for when examining actual historic clothing and other related aged objects.

Chapter 3

Fashion Snippets

It was a Friday morning in May, and I was busy at the university when the phone rang in my office. I answered it, and there was a woman on the other end of the line who was calling to ask me to come to her summerhouse. She mentioned that she was a long-time summer resident in the area, living in Boston the rest of the year, and said that I had been recommended to her. She wanted me to look at something she owned, saying that it was "very special." She also said that because it was something so precious, it was time to decide what to do with it. She told me that it "would be up to me," if she decided after the visit I would be the best person to receive it.

The woman sounded nice, if not a little bit demanding, but I was thinking that perhaps what she had to show me might possibly make a nice addition to our collection, and so I felt it worthy of my time to accept her invitation for a visit. She didn't want to wait until the following week, however, and pretty much insisted it be that very same day, saying, "Come for tea this afternoon." It seemed more like a summons than an invitation, but I thought perhaps I should accept. I was used to being contacted by people who were interested in our collection and had questions about their textiles. Most would make appointments and come to my office, and I always enjoyed helping them. However, sometimes people wanted me to go to see them, and this was one of those times. I would be late getting home to my family that night, but I would call ahead to let them know.

When I finished work for the day, I gathered up a few supplies and my briefcase and drove to the lady's house, following the directions she had given me over the phone. I really had no idea where I was going, not being familiar with the area, so I hoped they were good directions. Eventually they led me to a private drive off a main road and quite a way into the woods. I didn't see any indication of buildings for a while and nervously kept driving, until suddenly I saw a large house directly in front of me.

Relieved that I had found the prospective donor's residence, I parked where I had been instructed and walked up the pathway to the front entrance. Looming in front of me was a gigantic wooden door that had a large, round hand-forged doorknocker. I lifted the heavy knocker and rapped several times on the door. A few seconds later, a tall and older-looking woman in a plain cotton dress slowly opened the door and looked down at me. She seemed to be examining me. Then she asked me for my name, and after I told her who I was, she introduced herself as the person who had called me, nodded politely, and beckoned me into her front hall.

She kept walking, and I followed her until we came to a rather formal living room. Standing on one side of that large room as we entered were a gentleman well-dressed in black and white, and a lady wearing a black dress and a fancy, white tea apron. They were quite elderly, as I recall, and probably had been working for this lady for a long time. They both smiled and bowed politely as I entered the room and nodded and smiled. Then the lady of the house directed me to a large sofa, and the two of us sat down.

She and I chatted for about fifteen minutes while the maid and butler stood by at attention. Then deciding she liked me, I guess, she said to her servants, "I think we shall have scotch instead of tea," whereupon she turned to me and said, "Would that be acceptable to you?" It was long after work had ended officially for the day, so I felt it was acceptable, and not wanting to cause any discomfort, I replied that it would.

Her maid and butler left the room and returned shortly with silver trays containing glasses, ice, scotch, and some small crackers and napkins. They then nodded politely and left us to converse. We spent a good hour talking about history and some of her prominent ancestors, and even a few of mine, and then she ushered me into an adjoining room where her servants were now standing next to a large trunk. The lady said, "What is in this trunk is very important. It contains a bridal gown of one of my ancestors, worn in the mid-nineteenth century. She wed a prominent gentleman of note nearby." When she told me who they were, I recognized their names and was very excited. What a wonderful historic connection this gown would make to the collection at the university, I thought.

She had her butler open the trunk, and as he did, I put on a pair of cotton gloves I had brought to wear. Her maid helped me carefully lift a beautiful gown out of the trunk and place it on a clean sheet that I had brought with me. We discussed the gown and some history of the bride's wedding day in more detail, and I took lots of notes. The gown was made of silk and dyed a muted green color, with handmade lace trim, a tiny waist, and a full skirt, typical of the period. It was beautifully hand sewn and fully lined. I could imagine the young bride on her wedding day, perhaps with her hair in cascading curls, wearing a lovely lace bridal veil and a locket around her neck.

After a little more discussion, the lady did decide to donate the gown. It was now nighttime, and I had to say good-bye. I made an appointment to come back again so that I could prepare the donation for transport the next week when I would personally deliver it to the collection. Later I sent the donor an official acceptance letter and made sure the gown was properly boxed for storage in the collection at the university, where it remains a significant part of local history and a wonderful example of period fashion.

I was pleasantly surprised when I received a cordial note from the donor quite a while later. It was around Christmas. She sent me a lovely card with greetings for the season and a nice little letter. I was so glad to have had the opportunity to meet such an interesting individual.

This is one of the many experiences I had as a curator and remember fondly, not only because I found it interesting but also because I believe it is a good example of how precious pieces of fashion with historical significance sometimes are located, documented, and protected for future study.

I think we all enjoy a treasure hunt. Finding period clothing can be exciting and provides us with a source for questions. Today one may come across such objects as a top hat, vest, cravat, a pair of spats, or a bow tie for a groom or another gentleman from the early twentieth century, packed away and probably forgotten about years ago. And if one is really lucky and finds a trunk that was put away even longer ago, historic items that include garments and accessories from earlier centuries might be discovered. Perhaps one might find a man's frockcoat, a beaver hat, a pair of breeches, and maybe old buckles that had been worn on men's shoes or breeches. Whatever is found will generate our curiosity, making us want to learn more about it.

While thinking about all of this, I wrote a little poem you may find appropriate:

> *It was a gently worn top hat for ceremonies galore,*
> *For important state occasions, celebrations and more,*
> *Memories imbedded in its brim and crown,*
> *A treasure to own and a delight when found!*

Of course, many men in earlier America were hardworking farmers and would not have had large wardrobes. In most cases, they had just basic work clothes and maybe one dress outfit for church and state occasions. Their work clothes would wear out after a while and then would need to be mended. After many repairs and when they were no longer wearable, the castoff clothes might be saved for scraps for mending or for something else, such as a patchwork quilt. Nothing was wasted, but because of their clothing being mostly worn out and not saved, it has made it difficult to find men's whole work clothes from that time in history.

Because very little of men's work clothes have survived today intact, this makes them rare finds, and they are sometimes sought after by museums. Once in a while, an old pair of work trousers or a shirt surfaces, and one can see how carefully the shirt was mended and how the trousers were patched. Men's work pants might be patched with pieces of other textiles (a waste-not, want-not philosophy in practice), and as such they provide us with extra clues, hinting at what was being woven at home and what type of textiles were available to them. I have examined eighteenth-century work pants patched with handwoven pillow ticking and blanket fragments, illustrating what was available to one family for mending their clothing.

Because more women's and children's clothing than men's seemed to have been saved and mended to be used again, we find more of their garments today. It was not uncommon for women, especially those living on farms in earlier times in America (circa early 1700s to the mid-1800s), to have only owned one or two dresses. One would be for church and other special occasions, and another or maybe two for everyday wear during their long workdays. Farm life was hard, and it was no place for delicate, fancy, expensive garments. Unless women were of wealth and leisure, most could not afford such luxuries.

Fabric was expensive in the early years and often hard to acquire, much of the finer textiles having to be imported from abroad. Making clothing also took lots of time and skill. Cotton, linen, and woolen fabrics and blends were available for purchase but might be costly for a farm family. Furthermore, all of their fabrics could be produced on the farm if there were supplies, equipment, and time and energy to do so.

As mentioned, clothing wasn't in abundance on many farms, but people did the best they could to produce what they needed. A woman might make her dress over when she became pregnant, to fit better as she gained weight. Then she would reconvert the bodice later after the child was born, to try to make it look as nice and as functional as possible for feeding a new baby. When that was no longer necessary, the dress bodice could be redesigned again.

If women could not afford to buy a fancy dress and there was a newer fashion becoming popular, they might alter a dress to reflect the newer fashion. After wearing it for a while and the fashion having changed again, one might keep the dress and alter it once more, or it could be saved and used next by daughters or others in the family, or by a servant if there were any in the household.

And so, clothing in this country at that time reflects the lives of many different Americans, including those who worked on farms or in shops and also those of wealth who could afford more luxurious clothing. For the wealthier people, of course, there were tailors of note, creating fine fashion for those who demanded it. Many elegant, hand-tailored garments for women and men are still found today from this period, and the soft silks, satins, lush brocades, damasks, and other fabrics of such clothing are often beautiful.

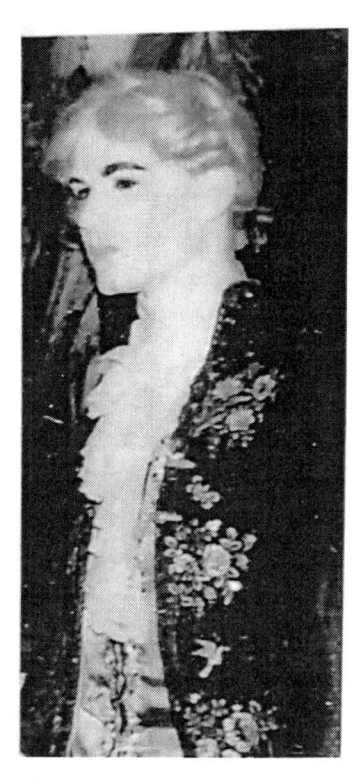

Figure 3. Detail of embroidery, gentleman's coat, late eighteenth century.

We want to discuss historic and vintage items now a little more carefully. I have included a little overview of several historic periods to help you understand more of what you may be looking at. Because some styles may be unrecognizable to you if you have little or no background in historic or vintage fashions, gaining some basic knowledge of various silhouettes and construction details of different periods can help provide clues when one attempts to date period fashions.

Fashions started to change, and clothing could be mass produced more easily and less expensively around the 1870s when sewing machines became more available. They had been used mostly by tailors and by workers in textile factories who were trained to use them. Around the turn of the century (ca. 1900), the country was changing rapidly, and the way people dressed was changing as well. They were starting to adjust to the new way they lived. We see more somber and efficient-looking fashion surviving from that later period. Many women had joined the work force, and many of the popular business-type, machine-made, white shirtwaist bodices, dresses, and long, dark-colored skirts and tops worn by the women of that era still survive today in collections.

The sewing machine had become more affordable for the average person, making it possible for more clothing to be made at home. Today when we examine garments from that period, we see that some of this clothing does not appear to be well made. It is most likely because the people who bought sewing machines to sew on at home were not proficient at using them. The machines probably seemed strange and must have been quite hard to operate at first by an untrained person. Stitching would be irregular, showing their lack of skill, which has actually helped, interestingly enough, making it easier for curators and others to properly date such garments to that particular time period when they were likely produced.

We also see much more ready-to-wear clothing that was made in factories. There may still be some hand stitching included in a garment, but now they are mostly machine made. We also are beginning to notice that the dark and very rich somber colors many had been wearing throughout the Victorian period are becoming less popular. It was the beginning of a new century, and with the advancement of new dyes, more bright and light colors and patterned designs would soon start entering the scene.

Fine designer clothing of course had different standards. Garments had special labels to identify the designer and were usually very costly. Some designers of note were gaining popularity because of the prominent individuals who chose to buy and wear their work. Fashion magazines were sought after by many people wanting to see such creations on display. Also popular were dress patterns that one could buy and use to make one's own garments.

Back in the time of the French Queen Marie Antoinette (1755–1793), Rose Bertin was the queen's dressmaker of note, and of course everything was made of very fine fabric for a queen. Even today, it is not unusual for royalty to employ dressmakers and fashion designers. In the 1920s and 1930s, many fashion designers were making names for themselves and had huge followings, but with WWII, things slowed down. Now there were clothing restrictions enforced by the government. One was not able to obtain fine designer fashions easily now, for they were not accessible. Most of the fashion houses were shut down for the duration, with very few open even in Europe. And any fashion houses allowed to remain open in Europe during the occupation were heavily controlled and accessible only to occupying forces.

During WWII, it is interesting to note that in America, there were actually heavy restrictions on how much fabric could be used to make clothing, along with restrictions on food, machinery, and more. When examining clothing from those years, it is quite intriguing to see the shortcuts manufacturers and others took to create garments and to make them look attractive with such limited resources. The war effort was in full force, and it was thought to be patriotic to be frugal and obey the restrictions. After the war, fashion picked up again, with designers back in business, creating beautiful designer originals for those who could afford them.

In the mid-twentieth century, some people were wearing garments made of paper. Not just regular paper but paper made with a little heavier texture, some of it containing cotton and other fibers that helped strengthen it. Garments were produced in silver or gold color for special use, some with advertising on them, and others were made to be party fashions like the go-go dress for dancing. You could redo the dress to adjust the length and even cut the paper with scissors to make fringe at the hem. It was all new and quite different to everyone then, and some of these paper dresses are collectibles today.

Many historic designer originals with famous labels are sought after by collectors now and command a very high price when sold. Numerous designer garments of note are in prominent museum collections throughout the world and are on exhibit to be viewed periodically. Imagine finding one of these in the trunk in the attic!

Many old clothing items and accessories have been donated or purchased by museums, collectors, and others to be protected, studied, and displayed. We also find that some fashions from the not too distant past have been displayed in travelling exhibitions. They contain designer originals created for famous individuals. One example would be that of Diana, Princess of Wales. Many find viewing garments that were worn and belonged to a princess, musician, actor, fashion model, dignitary, or some other well-known person, past or present, interesting, educational, and exciting.

Additionally, we find that some designer originals created by famous designers are prized for that reason alone and not just because a famous person might have worn them. I believe that all these garments should be given special attention, preferably under the care of trained professionals who understand the importance of protecting them for future generations.

Chapter 4

Bits and Pieces

It was a crisp early morning, and the two little girls had just finished breakfast. Their mother was bustling about making tea in the kitchen and told the girls she didn't want them underfoot, so they knew something interesting was about to happen. It was a sunny day, so they went outdoors and sat on their swings, and that was when they happened to see that there were many ladies approaching the front steps of their house.

The little girls watched intently for a moment, wondering what was happening and why, and then leaving their swings, they started walking back to the house. That was when they saw their father bringing the quilting frame equipment out of the barn. He walked past the little girls, bringing all the pieces of the frame into the house, and put everything on the floor in the front parlor.

Peeking into the room, the girls quietly watched their father set up the quilting frame. They were sure now that this was for all the ladies who had come to visit. Then, when their father had finished putting the frame together, he turned around, and seeing the two little girls across the room, he went over to them and happily hugged them. Then he looked down at them and told them to have a nice time and to be good girls and said that he was going to go to work. And as they waved good-bye, he left.

Meanwhile, their mother's friends were helping her bring in all the sewing materials to prepare for the day's activity. The girls were excited now, for they knew that a quilting bee was about to begin! Standing on the steps near the front door, the two little ones attentively watched everything unfold and thought it fun to see everyone so cheerful.

Once everything was set up, their mother said that the girls could come back into the house if they wanted to but that they were not allowed to sit with the ladies because they were too young. However, their mother remarked that if they were very quiet, they could play nearby while the ladies quilted. That was okay at first of course, but eventually the girls got a little restless, and their toys no longer keeping them occupied, they decided that they wanted to watch the ladies more closely as they sewed.

They noticed that there was much conversation among the grown-ups, and the girls thought it sounded like they all had an awful lot to talk about. They evidently were very involved and enjoying the day. The room seemed very active too, with everybody sewing on such a big quilt. The ladies were all spaced out with the quilt stretched in front of them on the large frame, which was rectangular in shape. The quilt was rolled under on two sides. It appeared gigantic to the little girls, and it certainly seemed like everything took up a huge amount of room.

Eventually, after having had several small conversations with some of the ladies, the girls felt that they had discussed the quilting process pretty thoroughly, and so they decided that they didn't need to ask any more questions for now. They sat together for a while and had fun playing with their cat, Old Bill, and then they wondered what to do next. They thought about going outside to have fun on their swings, but then looking back at the huge quilt, the two of them decided that they would walk closer and look underneath it. When they did that, they realized that there was lots of room under there and that it might be a perfect place for them to play house! They decided they needed to explore the space more thoroughly, and so they quietly went farther under to get an even better look.

They liked it so much that they agreed to make it their very own special place for the day. And with all the talking in the room, no one would be the slightest bit aware that the two of them might be under there, for the ladies were all busy sewing and enjoying one another's company above the quilt.

The girls went out from under the quilt and merrily gathered up their toys and books and their cat. They brought them all back underneath the quilt to play with, happy to have their own special place. No one above the quilt had the slightest idea that the children were under there all morning long, until it was their nap time, and that was when their mother discovered their secret!

Figure 4. Author's sketch of an early quilting frame.

What you just read is a little story from the past with glimpses of a quilting bee, which was a fairly popular activity in earlier times in America. It would be planned carefully and enjoyed in homes, serving both as a practical and a social occasion, mostly from the late

1700s through the early 1900s, and there may even be more than a few still happening today.

Quilts have often been treasured as special home furnishings and much admired. A bride's hope chest might contain quilts she made, showing her needle skills. A new bride or bride-to-be might also be presented with one made at a quilting party. Many old quilts today seem to have a story to tell, especially if we are looking very closely at them. We may find ourselves wondering what kind of garments the pieces of fabric came from originally and who might have owned them. One might think of early quilts as a mirror into the past in a way, for they seem to call our attention to their popular patterns and colors of a bygone day. When we look at them, we can also imagine how they must have looked when they adorned an early four-poster bed. Some women and men are still making quilts, and although a few are made for utilitarian purposes, many are primarily created as works of art today.

Many find quilts interesting, whether old or new. An early quilt usually consisted of two large sections with a center filling. Some were joined by being tied or quilted together with a center filling, such as cotton batting, although not all had fillings. Some had a blanket or sheeting in between, which provided more warmth, making it not only heavier but more comfortable for a cold winter.

The top layer of a pieced or patchwork quilt was usually made with many small bits and pieces of textiles sewn together. Some were done in a pattern, and others at random. The bottom layer often was made of a solid piece of fabric and might be just plain, white cotton or linen, although some were quite decorative, printed in different patterns. Earlier ones may sport a wood-block or copperplate printed fabric. Today when we look at quilts created in the late 1700s to middle 1800s, we can see the craftsmanship and skill of those who produced the hand-blocked and early machine-printed fabrics in many of them.

Quilts often had descriptive types of pattern names, such as Streaks of Lightning, Flower Garden, Nine Patch, Log Cabin, or Honeycomb. They may have been made for a special occasion or celebration, such as for a wedding or some kind of fraternal organization, as well as to be decorative or practical. There were many quilts that were created for many different reasons. Some quilts are signed, and others are not. I think it is always exciting to find one that is signed, especially if it might give some information that could help date it, and if there is a name or date on a quilt, one might be able to find out more about the original owner.

Another early household furnishing that I want to mention is the appliqued quilt. Applique bedcovers were quite popular, and many a lady demonstrated her needle skills creating a floral design or by copying one from a pattern onto a textile. The top would usually have a plain ground, although not always, with different pieces of cut shapes of fabrics forming a design, sewn on its surface. Some appliqued quilts I find are very beautiful and quite artistic with floral designs and vines and other delicate figures, birds, etc.

Some quilts have lots of hand embroidery and could be delicate or quite elaborate and colorful. Others might contain words, phrases, names, and dates, along with flowers, birds, and such. Some of these are also quilted in sections as part of the design.

Figure 5. Detail of appliqued design, hand quilted.

Some are also ceremonial. I have one that my grandmother made for my grandfather. It has appliqued Masonic symbols on it and some quilting, although the bright red symbols are the most dominant part of the design.

Figure 6. Hand-sewn quilt with Masonic insignia, circa 1910.

Crazy quilts from the Victorian period display the wonderful richness of colors from that period in their designs, and I find them exciting and often quite interesting. A multitude of precious and colorful fragments were sewn onto palettes of textile sheeting or light blanket fabric to create these works of art. They were often embellished with embroidered inscriptions, designs, or figures, or perhaps all three, done in brilliantly colored silk thread, making them very artistic.

While curator at URI, I researched a quilt that was made by an elderly gentleman long ago. (Not only women have made quilts.) This interesting quilt was made from many pieces of satin, probably saved from men's ties, and was done in a cobweb design. Looking at these objects now makes one curious about what the textile fragments had been part of before they were just bits and pieces.

Crazy quilts beautified Victorian homes and were often displayed on the bed or draped over a piece of furniture, a piano, or on a wall.

Some of these creations are exhibited in museums today, and others are seen in present-day homes as gently used furnishings, displayed as art, or cherished and passed down as part of a family history.

There are still other types of quilts. If you find one in a chest that is not pieced, it might be a linsey-woolsey quilt. It was one of the earliest quilts made in America and is more often found in colder climates like New England. It was woven with a linen warp and a wool weft. The quilt top was made of a fine linsey-woolsey, and the bottom usually of a homespun fabric of linen or cotton. It had layers that were quilted together, and the middle usually was of a thin woolen fabric. Some petticoats worn by women and girls for the winter weather also would be made of linsey-woolsey, for it is a heavy and warm fabric. Petticoats of this type might also be quilted. Quilting was used in many ways and for many centuries. It even was worn under armor long ago.

There was another type of whole cloth quilted bedcover called white work, or trapunto. It was not pieced to create a design. The major difference between white work and the linsey-woolsey quilts was that this one was more delicate and always had only two layers. The top was of a fine, white cotton fabric, and the bottom of a homespun cotton or linen. The hand-sewn designs usually are more decorative than those of linsey-woolsey quilts, and the stitches smaller and tighter. The homespun layer is of a loose weave, making it possible to stuff a filling, usually of soft cotton, into the quilted design sections from underneath, using a bodkin or other such implement. This was done to form a sculptured look to the pattern after the bedcover top was designed and both sections were sewn together.

In addition to those types already mentioned, you may come across something that looks like a bedcover of sorts. It could be (if you are very lucky) that you have found what was called a bed rug, or a "wrap rascal," and it is quite rare today. Some were sturdy and some very decorative, according to my research, and they might be used not only to decorate a bed but also to be placed on the floor, on a table, or even to serve as a warm blanket. I actually saw one at one point in my work and was able to examine it closely. It was rather loosely woven but nicely done. It had a neutral ground with a simple floral design in its center and a border of smaller flowers. I thought it was fascinating because it put me in touch with something rare that was enjoyed by our ancestors. Looking at it at the time, I felt like I was back in the eighteenth century.

I find that some of the terminology confuses people at times. Often a textile that is not constructed into a structured garment or other such object is referred to as a "flat textile" by curators. Although "costume" is a word used in the profession rather than "clothing," a flat textile can also be a piece of costume (clothing) that still is referred to as being a flat textile if it is a wearable, flat piece of fabric. Some flat textiles may not serve as a wrap, a part of a garment, or another type of accessory, but be an object that is part of a home furnishing treatment such as a table cover, sheet, drapery, tapestry, etc.

Delving into some historical background in books or on the Internet, you may find that you recognize similar objects that will help you learn about how the ones you have found were used. I can't of course go into great detail on everything that is in existence here in this little book, so I have jotted down a few points for you, to give you clues that may help you in figuring out how some flat textiles were used if you find one or more in your search.

There are many types of flat textiles, in addition to the bedcovers and other flat textiles we have already talked about. For example, you may find silk damasks or brocades or a textile that was created to be a chair seat cover, tapestry, or other wall decoration. Many beautiful textiles contain patterns and metallic thread, and some are covered with embroidery, and so forth, depending on their intended use.

When you look into that trunk you found, you may also discover that there are lots of different types of flat textiles that were put away long ago as yardage. Because people did a lot of hand sewing and many made their own clothes, you may find that you have some of what they were saving to maybe make into clothing later on. Sometimes previously used fine fabric from pieces of clothing were saved to be recycled. There may be fragments or actual shaped pieces that look like they were parts of former garments, and of course they probably were, for fabric was expensive and valued.

There are many reasons why textiles are a prominent part of our everyday life. Asking how they were manufactured and why are questions that can provide interesting answers. We find many justifications for why we need to include textiles of all types when we see the many innovations that have been created since our early beginnings in the industry, including the Slater Mill in Pawtucket, Rhode Island. We can do our research, and then we will certainly see that there have been many changes and advancements in how textiles were produced, moving from natural fibers to synthetics and beyond.

Figure 7. Slater Mill—first cotton-spinning factory in America, 1793.

Chapter 5

All Natural

I remember one day in particular when I was a young teenager, walking through the meadows on our farm with my dog. The sun was shining brightly, and it seemed to add a sparkle to all the trees and wildflowers and even our sheep grazing in the nearby fields.

Everything seemed so fresh and alive. The sheep were really enjoying the weather too, I mused. I looked at them from across the field and noticed how thick their wool was, and just for a moment I thought it looked like cake frosting or maybe whipped cream. They had so much wool. I knew they would soon be sheared. I knew that every year there was a shearing and that the wool was sent to a co-op my parents belonged to. On our beds, my little sister and brother and I all had nice, thick blankets made from that wool to keep us warm.

Finally, the day arrived. The shearing began early in the morning. It was late afternoon now, and my father had been very busy most of the day tending to our flock of sheep, shearing one at a time near the barn. My mother had been helping him, and I had been attentively watching the whole process from the other side of the fence. Nearly all our sheep had been sheared and had gone back out to pasture through the wide, wooden gate beside the barn.

It had been a long day but was kind of interesting, I thought as I gazed out over the fields. Then, I noticed that there was one sheep left to shear. While I was looking at it, my father suddenly turned around and beckoned to me. He knew I had been watching, and to my great surprise, he asked me if I wanted to help him shear the last one. That was the first time he had ever asked! Of course I eagerly told him I would, thinking that it might be fun. (He probably was thinking it would be a good experience.) My mother decided that since the shearing was almost finished, she would go into the house to start making dinner. I happily climbed over the fence into the field to join my father.

And so we began. With the ewe turned on her side and her hooves in the air, my father showed me how to hold on to her so he could shear her. I held her under her forearms and leaned her against my legs as instructed. My father was being very careful with the shears so as to not hurt the ewe, and I held her as tightly as I could to keep her still. I watched closely as my father skillfully worked the shears to try to keep the fleece in one whole piece. I knew that securing a whole fleece was preferable but not an easy thing to do.

I was thinking happily to myself that I was glad my father let me help him. Then, just when he was almost finished removing the fleece, I thought something seemed to be tightening around my ankle. I wondered if maybe I was just imagining it, but now it seemed to be that something was tightening around my jeans, squeezing my right leg. It wasn't my imagination! I looked nervously downward, still holding on to the sheep, and that was when I saw a large, black snake looking up at me! I screamed! The snake, most likely equally frightened (he probably screamed too), hurriedly unwrapped himself from my leg and quickly slithered off into the high grass while the sheared ewe trotted off in the opposite direction.

Of course my heart was pounding loudly, for I was really scared, but I tried hard to calm down. My father realized what had happened and appeared a little stunned at first (but I thought for a moment I saw him smiling), while he took a second or two to look at the scurrying snake before he looked back at me. He then casually told me that I was not to worry because black snakes don't bite people, and besides, it probably just thought I was a tree. That of course calmed me down some, and I really did feel better. Unforgettably, that was my first really close-up adventure, so to speak, with freshly sheared wool.

I suppose a lot of us wear a piece of clothing or cuddle up in a warm, woolen blanket without being too concerned about what it is made of or how it was produced. Many of us also go about our busy lives not thinking about how we got to be where we are today. I think if each one of us were to stop and ponder how much we take for granted, we might realize how little we know about such things. Then again, perhaps if we really did think about it, we would see how certain things from the past have had an influence on us, making a difference in our lives. A lot certainly has happened to bring us to where we are, even when we are talking about textiles.

In the early days in America, producing a blanket or other woolen textile was often done from start to finish on the farm. The sheep were sheared, and the wool was cleaned, combed, and then spun on a spinning wheel or by using a drop spindle. The handspun yarn was then readied to be put on a loom where a family member would weave the fabric, or an itinerant weaver might be hired to do the work.

The weaver used a pattern draft to set up the warp and the weft. The width of the loom determined the width of the fabric. Some clothing pieces and rugs and other objects woven might require only one loom width. However if the fabric was for something needing more width, such as a large bed, a longer length would be woven in the pattern and then cut into two pieces (or more) and matched and sewn together. Some examples include sheets, blankets, coverlets, portieres, and large rugs.

One of my first major publications was about a weaver who lived in Rhode Island (1840–1915). He was very interesting to me because several coverlets that had once been woven by him were part of a collection I had worked with as part of my earlier thesis research. William Henry Harrison Rose was his name, but he was better known locally as Weaver Rose. Wonderful coverlets were hand woven by Weaver Rose and his sister Elsie on handlooms on their farm, which was not far from where the University of Rhode Island is today in Kingston, Rhode Island.

A coverlet is a type of handwoven bedcover that you might find in a chest or trunk. It is usually a fairly heavy textile, handwoven in a geometric-looking pattern on a loom. The coverlet usually has a linen warp (threads run lengthwise) and a wool weft (threads run widthwise), although some have been woven with a cotton warp. Linen is strong, but wool takes to dyes better than linen does, so dyeing the yarns made of wool for the weft and having the white linen yarn for the warp produced bright patterns. Dark blue was a popular color, and I have seen many blue and white coverlets. Colors used included dark brown, yellow, orange, and others, and several colors might have been used to create a particular pattern. Many pattern drafts were created by weavers and handed down through generations and have whimsical names, such as Bachelor's Fancy, Cat Tracks in the Wilderness, and Orange Peel.

Figure 8. Loom for hand weaving, early to mid-nineteenth century.

It took a while to weave a coverlet, and there were a number of itinerant weavers travelling from town to town, weaving coverlets as a profession. The weaver would set up his loom or use the owner's loom on the farm to do the work. The weaver usually would have a selection of patterns to show a customer, and I have actually seen a number of these in my research. Sometimes woven samples were made by a weaver and were tied together to form a booklet of sorts. They might also be put on a metal ring that would keep them together for potential customers to choose from. They held small sample pieces of coverlets, with squares of the different designs showing what the patterns looked like. There are some that still survive today, containing old pattern drafts.

There were also drafts written on sheets of paper. Weaver Rose had quite an assortment of handwritten pattern drafts. I remember seeing an old photograph showing a paper with the pattern draft on it that was being woven, pinned above the old-fashioned wooden loom that the weaver was working on. (Part of my research involved attending a weaving institute to learn how to weave, read drafts, and produce a coverlet using one of Weaver Rose's pattern drafts.)

Once a design or pattern draft was chosen and the coverlet woven at home by family members or by an itinerant weaver, it became an important household object to be put to good use. It adorned a bed, covered one's knees on a cold day while riding in a carriage or sled, or served as a thick coverlet or bed rug (which was called a "wrap rascal" in one weaver's letters I studied). Today, we may see some of these handwoven coverlets for sale in antique shops or in homes on display, perhaps draped gently over a rack in front of a bed. They are also occasionally displayed as works of art in galleries and museums to be admired and enjoyed.

Figure 9. Handwoven coverlets, late nineteenth century.

Now I shall discuss another type of natural fiber textile you may come across in your search for treasures. I remember learning in my research that early on in this country there was an attempt to produce silk in New England. Mulberry trees were planted. The purpose was to feed silkworms, their food being mulberry leaves. Silkworms produced cocoons, and the silk was harvested from the cocoons and spun. However, it was short-lived here, the climate not being constant and suitable for such an endeavor. There may still be a few pieces of locally manufactured silk fabric in existence from that time, but, if so, I imagine they would be a rare find.

Linen was much easier to produce than silk in America. Farmers would plant their crop of flax and harvest it. The flax would be processed using a hackle to help break it down and soften it, and the fibers combed lengthwise and spun on a spinning wheel. The spun yarns were then made ready for the loom. Lots of clothing, bed linens, and other textiles were made from linen. It was strong and wore well. I still see many men's shirts of linen that have survived from the eighteenth century. Sometimes linen and wool were combined, as mentioned previously, in the quilts called linsey-woolsey. Some recreated villages have interpreters demonstrating the production of woolen and linen textiles. Natural fiber fabrics also include cotton, which was grown mostly in the southern states early on. After cotton was harvested, cleaned, and readied, it was sent out to cotton mills where lots of colorful textiles were produced.

Natural fiber fabrics were dependent on their physical characteristics and treatment, and use was determined by their limitations. Manmade textile fibers (i.e., rayon) were developed in the early twentieth century and had their own particular defining features. For example, when weighted silks were created, they had a brilliance or sheen that contributed to their appearance because of the process that involved the addition of mineral salts, but most of these textiles have not held up well over time. Some synthetics and other finishes that were developed were produced by using a number of different chemical treatments, and we can see that some of the colors are more vivid, and some of the textiles are stronger and behave differently.

When we find vintage clothing items that are not from the really distant past, we often find they are made of blends. Some may be of natural and synthetic fabrics that are combined in the same garment. Processes are constantly changing, sometimes making it harder to date an aged textile or garment. Not every process used in a textile causes the same kind of reaction the same way over time, and one may need to do more research in order to date the textile properly. This is a time when knowing textile history is especially helpful. Natural fibers and fabrics can be processed better today, changing their performance capabilities, which can have an effect on the type of care needed. Care instructions in or on present-day garments and other textile objects are helpful and did not exist much earlier.

So, we see how confusing it can all be. As mentioned, I find that one can more easily date such objects if the style of the garment represents a fashion from a particular period. But there are other methods. Unless it is a serious project, using fashion history is a good beginning. We can see how much has changed, and as we watch, we can see how it continues to do so, but I think it is interesting that we still find natural fiber fabrics being used today, regardless.

Now you can see that our country has gone in cycles where natural fiber fabrics are sought after and where synthetics have taken favor. Interestingly enough, at the moment, we are enjoying all of them.

To sort of summarize, I look at it this way. Today many people prefer the natural fabrics but have to remember that they may need to be ironed, and some may even need to be dry-cleaned. There are also lots of synthetics and blends, and they don't seem to need nearly as much care. Today we also have care labels to help us identify fiber content and to give us care instructions, and they can be very helpful. We must remember that our lifestyle often makes the decisions for us (for example, how much time we have to take care of the clothes we wear and those we want to keep).

When doing research on aged textiles that are of natural fibers, I like to mention that one must be careful to not be fooled. Just because it is of natural fibers does not mean it is an early piece. Key for identification is the textile, fashion silhouette, construction, and any other specific details that may help you date it. Remember too that synthetics differed early on and that you should look for signs that may indicate it is an earlier synthetic rather than a newer one. Color fastness may even be a clue, and finishes also need to be considered. Again, remember that one can go to the library or check online when searching for more information on any of this.

Chapter 6

Summer Heat

It was Sunday, and the church was full. The weatherman had said that it was going to be a warm day, and I noticed that some of the ladies were sporting colorful straw hats with wide brims. As I looked across the aisle, I happened to see a young teenage girl who appeared to be about fifteen or sixteen years old, holding a beautiful fan. It certainly was an antique, and I was surprised to see it in church. The fan was quite large and had beautiful ostrich plumes of white. The sticks appeared to be of delicate, pierced ivory with a painted floral design, and the fan was trimmed with a blue silk cord and tassel. While gazing at the fan, I imagined it being at an opera many years before, held in the gloved hand of a fine lady in an elegant gown.

While I sat in my pew admiring the fan and wondering why someone would bring it to church instead of displaying it carefully in a case at home, the young girl started waving the fan back and forth across her face. I guess she was very warm, and the fan was cooling her. Whenever I happened to look in her direction, however, I was a little concerned, because my curator-trained mind couldn't stop worrying about that fan.

All during the service, the fan was waved about while the young lady joyfully opened and closed it. And to my dismay, sometimes she even closed it in reverse. By the expression on her face, she seemed to really love her fan. She just didn't understand that she was harming it.

Of course I was not able to speak to her because I was sitting too far away, but I wished that I could have. By the end of the sermon, the fan was looking quite disturbed, the plumes somewhat tangled and puffy.

Finally the service was over, and as we all filed out of the church, I thought I would try to get close enough to her to get her attention and speak with her. When I did, I said that I had noticed her lovely antique fan, thereby hoping to start a little conversation. I wanted to explain to her that it was very old and gently suggest that it might be better not opened and closed so much and why. She was in a hurry to catch up with her friends that she had been sitting with in the church, and so we did not have much time to talk. As she turned back to look at me, she was smiling broadly at my compliment on her fan. She waved and said, "Thank you so much!" as she and her fan rushed out the door.

I had hoped to gently explain the nature of the fan and its age to the young lady, but that was not to be. Later on, I thought about the whole situation and wondered why she didn't realize she was causing damage to the fan that she seemed to like so much. Then I thought about it a little more and realized that because it was so beautiful, she most likely did not think of it as really old or fragile. I sometimes wonder if that fan is still in existence even though it was only a short time ago. If so, I am sure the young lady is enjoying it. But I do wish I could have given her some gentle advice.

We shall begin this chapter discussing the individual owner and his or her collection of historic textile objects. Like our young teenager in the story, not everyone realizes how age can affect an old textile or other aged object. There are many different motives that people have for collecting family heirlooms. Some just love their beauty and want to keep them for special occasions. Others collect them for investment purposes, for personal use, for display, or perhaps even to create an interesting piece of artwork. Whenever asked, I always advise that the owner do a little research and identify the period of the treasure before using it for anything, so that the owner will have a better understanding of what it is.

If it is a garment and is in very poor condition, one may use parts of it for something else or keep a piece of decorative ribbon, lace, or any other trim or a piece of the actual textile. One may also decide to do a series of drawings or photographs of the garment for a record. This especially might be good to do when an interesting garment or textile is badly damaged with no chance of restoring it. Some people have saved old buttons and mounted them for display or even made jewelry out of them, such as earrings or bracelets. I have always been a little dismayed when I see such jewelry and silently mourn for the garment they came from, probably because of being a curator.

There are many reasons for collecting historic or vintage textiles, costumes, and other related objects. Prominent among these ideas is the one of wearing a vintage garment as part of a celebration or as a costume. Some people like to collect and wear their treasures. However, there is much to be aware of when one decides to wear or use an aged garment or other textile object or accessory, and I believe that careful handling is at the top of the list.

Being of some age, many old textiles and related objects have various combinations of materials as well as other factors to consider that may indicate the need for special treatment. Not only do the age and materials come into play, but any number of things might affect the treatment of the object and need to be examined if one is attempting to enhance it in its present condition. I shall discuss some typical situations and observations that one may have when dealing with aged textiles, in order to give you some ideas of what you might want to consider when you first come in contact with them.

Because old textiles do not always look their age, it is important that one understands that they may be quite dry and brittle, especially if they were discovered in an area with exposure to heat and light. Therefore, one needs to examine these objects carefully before handling them, and common sense comes into play if you think about it.

I have illustrated to others how wrinkles might affect a textile, for example, by showing someone what happens when one crumples up a piece of ordinary paper and then opens it up again and tries to smooth it out. If you did this, you would see that the paper still has creases in it, like a textile that has been crumpled up in a trunk or somewhere else for a very long time or perhaps had something heavy on it while in storage. It would be hard to smooth the paper or the textile, and you might burn it if you tried to remove the wrinkles by ironing it. You might spray it first with a fine mist of distilled water to humidify it, which might help some, but it still would be damaged and probably show some hairline creases. And it might suffer from being sprayed if the dyes are not permanent in the textile, so that would also need consideration.

My favorite example I like to use when talking about handling aged textiles involves a brittle object. In a very exaggerated but perhaps easy-to-understand way, one might consider that a fragile old textile could be thought of as being almost as delicate or brittle as a potato chip. Once broken like a potato chip, the textile fabric cannot easily, if at all, be put back together. There are methods to explore but in many cases that would be true, especially if there is a bad break in the fabric. One may only see a slight difference looking at a wrinkled fabric quickly, but under a microscope you would see the breakage clearly.

Remember that although the fiber breakage may be hard to see with the naked eye, the damage is still there, and how it is treated when handled may determine whether it can be repaired or not. I believe when an aged textile object has deep creases or folds with visible wear, or actual voids or holes in places, it is best to assume that the fabric is fragile and deal accordingly.

Depending on the particular object, there are treatments that I would consider to protect the damaged areas. For example, I might remove the damaged or deteriorated sections and replace them with new fabric so that the object can be used as before, which might be good if it is not a significant object and is being used as a costume piece. If it is an important museum-quality piece, however, I would choose a different method. A careful overlay of a sheer, nonreactive fabric might be the solution in some situations, depending on the condition. This will help to mask or support the damaged or missing area of a garment or other object that is to be placed on exhibit. Under certain circumstances, it may be one of a few ways to safely display a significant historic garment or fragile textile that contains damage, but it must be done carefully.

It is not often that an aged garment is displayed in the home, although it does happen occasionally, and in that situation some of the same would apply. A glass cabinet or another type of glass case may be used at home for smaller objects, such as a lace collar or a fan, for example. These can be researched, and you will see that some museums have them. When buying a glass case, it is important to ask if the case is a museum-quality display piece. Lighting and the actual components of the case are important as well.

When it is a fragile, aged article of clothing to be worn again for something special, and it needs to be altered, one needs to be very careful when altering it. I might decide I want to construct a liner for the person to wear under it. This helps protect the aged garment from being stressed by movement from a wearer while one is enclosed in it. Of course it would depend on the condition, but even if altering is not necessary, I find that a liner often is a big help. A baby's christening gown or dress passed down in a family to be used again, or even a period wedding gown, is better protected that way.

If I have an aged garment that is no longer wearable, but I want to keep it regardless, I may measure each part of the garment carefully and make an actual copy of it and save it, in case I can find another use for it. Other times, an aged item may have too much damage to be restored to wear or put on display, but it may have some pieces of fabric that have remained in good condition, and if it is not possible to repair the garment, I might consider saving these remnants for other purposes. Many fine silks and satins retain their beauty over the years, and if the garment or other object is no longer useful as is, the remnants might be creatively used or recycled. When looking at patchwork quilts and Victorian crazy quilts from the past, we can see that people often made good use of such scraps.

Some people have family memorabilia of sorts to display in their homes, and that can take many forms. It could be a special textile, or a beautiful hat that a favorite grandmother wore long ago, or a delicate piece of lace in a frame that is hanging on a wall, or maybe a doll dressed in an outfit that sits in a rocking chair in a bedroom, or anything else of a similar nature. Some basic things to remember are that light can be damaging to a textile and that over time dust and heat and sun can further age it and cause more deterioration. If an object is on display in your home, try to keep this in mind. Cooking odors, tobacco smoke, and some air fresheners might also be problematic. When I display handmade lace or any other treasure, I try to be sure that it is not in a bright area or where there are fumes or dampness.

Framed textiles usually fare better if they are mounted professionally, if one can afford to have them done by a company that specializes in such work. Acid-free board and UV glass are some materials used by professionals.

In some homes, there are antique chairs that have old satin or needlepoint cushions that are lovely to look at but fragile if sat on. Such a mistake can be costly if the weight of a person causes the textile to split (or breaks the chair). To keep aged pieces of furniture and furnishings attractive but protected, I may drape a piece of fabric or some other attractive object on part of it so that no one will be tempted to sit on it. For example, it may be a pretty lace handkerchief or a paisley shawl, depending on the size of the furniture. This will act as a gentle visual barrier.

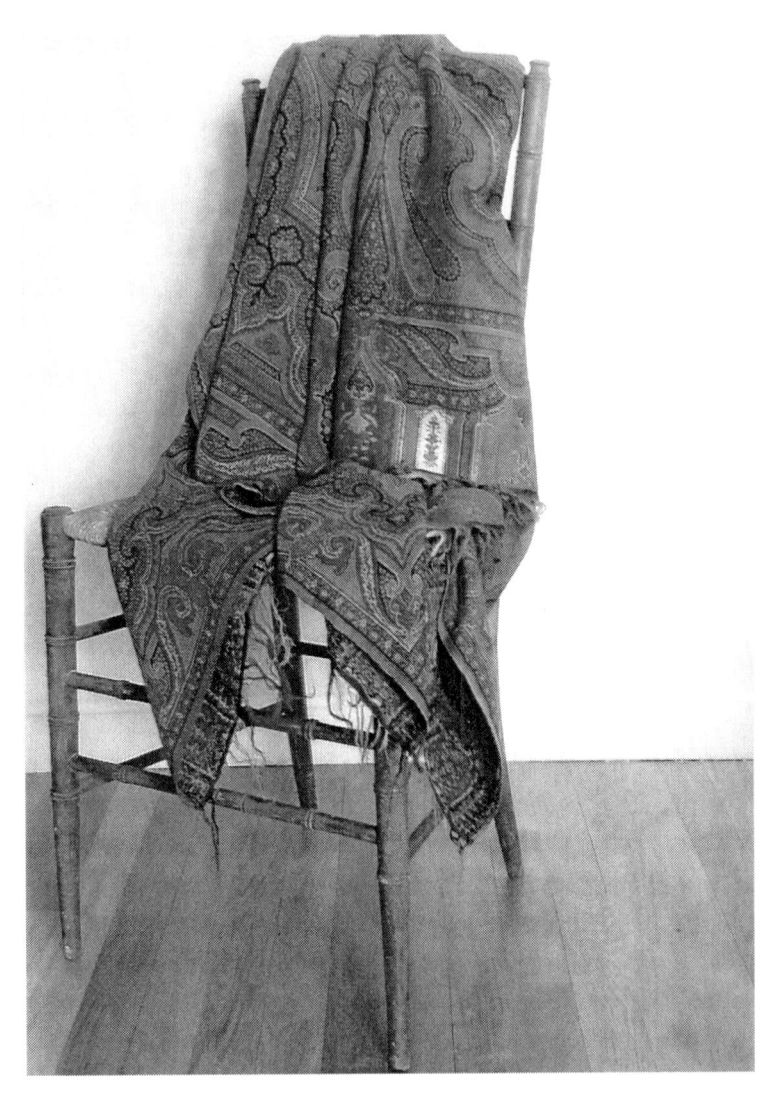

Figure 10. Early nineteenth-century chair, draped with a paisley shawl.

Even a lightweight and attractive, artificial, potted plant or small flower arrangement could work to help protect something, but make sure such objects have no sharp edges. If your object on display is going to be where people can reach it, a visual barrier is a gentle way of conveying to the viewer that touching or sitting on a particular object is not to be attempted. A lot of this is common sense, and I always stress that one just needs to think about such things step by step, using common sense as a guide.

Caution with placement in a home applies to many other aged home furnishings as well. One might find a quilt that would look wonderful on one's bed. However, be aware that if used like a new quilt, it could split or get torn easily as one tosses about in sleep, and then it could be ruined or at least need some restoration. There are decorative quilt and coverlet frames available that people put at the foot of the bed to drape the antique quilt over when going to bed. The frame protects the quilt nicely all night, and then it can be put back on the bed for display during the day.

Wall hangings, tapestries, and other textiles that are to be displayed on a wall need protection too. First they need to be carefully examined to be sure they are in good enough condition to be put on display. A wall hanging needs to be displayed on a proper rod and in a safe location that is free from handling, strong light, and fumes. Whether or not I use a liner, I sew a casing of muslin on the back of the piece for inserting a rod. If the casing is to be removable, basting stitches are used, and if not, a more permanent casing is carefully sewn on. I also find that a well-designed liner helps to keep a wall hanging from sagging and protects it from any dampness on a wall. Of course one should also remember to remove the hanging periodically for cleaning. There are other methods used, and one will want to do research and choose the best one for the project.

Figure 11. Casing example for textile display.

Remember that objects sometimes react with the environment they are in, so you want to be sure they are in a suitable location. Note again that when you are looking for ideas, it can be helpful to visit museums and other institutions when they are displaying textiles, to gather some information and ideas before displaying your own.

Chapter 7

Oh No!

It was a busy day, and I was involved in a quilt documentation project. People were being asked to bring their quilts to a specific location I had arranged for the project so that quilts from the area could be recorded and then photographed. The morning had certainly seemed to be a very productive one with the many quilts examined so far, and while observing the activities, I thought it especially interesting how some people handled their quilts. Some were careful of course, but others might drag their bag along the floor when they entered the room, especially if they had a very large, full bag. Then after their quilts had been documented and they found out how much interest others had in them, I noticed that those same people carried their quilts out of the room with extra care.

While I was thinking about how well the day was proceeding, one woman came over to the examining table where I was documenting quilts. She had a rather sad look on her face. When she lifted the bag containing her quilt onto the table and opened it, it was obvious that the quilt was not in good condition. The woman quietly told me that she was feeling a little upset about how her quilt looked and wanted to know what she had done wrong. She said she had wanted it to look as good as possible when she brought it to the documentation that day, but now she felt it was ruined. I looked at the quilt, which was a hand-sewn patchwork quilt done in the pattern called Streaks of Lightning. It was still together but barely.

I asked the woman to tell me what had happened and told her that I would try to help her. To offer her some comfort, I said that she certainly was not alone and that sometimes well-meaning people attempting to improve aged textile items just don't realize how fragile they are. I told her that it is because they usually don't have enough understanding of aged textiles that they are disappointed when they try to improve them, and their good intentions fail. She turned to me, looking somewhat guilty, and told me that "the quilt just looked like it needed a little freshening up," and that was why she had decided to wash it. She said that she was very careful and put the washing machine on the gentle cycle and used cold water because the quilt was quite old. She thought it would be okay but had trouble getting it out of the washer, and when she did remove the quilt, it was all "bunched up." She thought that if she put it in the dryer, it might "fluff it up."

Trying to not appear too shocked by the poor quilt's condition, I examined it carefully and noted that there was a thick filler or padding between the two outer layers of the quilt. I gently explained to her that very likely it had become extremely heavy when wet because it had absorbed too much water. Then I told her that it had expanded to a point where pressure caused by the expansion of the filling and the agitation of the washer, in addition to the dryer rotations, had weakened the aged, outer textile fabrics even more. These were major factors for why her antique quilt was now in such poor condition.

The lady seemed to understand, but it was an old family piece, and she was still quite upset about what she had done to it, as you can imagine. We talked for a while longer, and I went into a little more detail on what had happened to her quilt. I wanted to make sure that she understood what had occurred and why, so that hopefully it wouldn't happen again, for she said she had several more quilts at home. She thanked me and left, promising to bring in one of her old quilts she had not washed, later on that day.

Now that you have been introduced to some of the characteristics of aged textiles, clothing, and other related objects, I would like to give you a little more detailed information regarding the handling of such objects. We shall discuss examples that one may find fairly typical with aged textiles and some situations that you may even have perhaps experienced at one time or another. I shall present various types of problems and my solutions, to help you be more aware of what to think about when dealing with aged textiles.

Again, the age should always be considered carefully when judging how to treat such objects. Just imagine for a moment how you might feel if you were as fragile as a vintage garment or another aged textile item and were being treated or handled poorly. Might not you find that you would prefer more gentle treatment? When we think of treatment for the old textile object and the fabric itself, we must try to remember that unlike the human body, the old textile object does not have the same ability to rejuvenate or heal, and any improper repair or stress to such an object will likely cause permanent damage. Improper care might even destroy the beauty of the object for all time.

A major problem for those who are new to working with aged textiles is that the object might not look fragile, even though it is. An old textile is often in jeopardy because, to the untrained eye, it may appear to be in good condition, thereby causing one to treat it in the same manner as one would a new textile. Improper handling can damage it. It is important, therefore, to remember that how such an object looks to the naked eye may be deceiving, and one needs to always use caution when dealing with old textiles.

As a curator, I find it interesting that very often when people purchase an old garment or textile, or remove one from storage, intending to display or wear it, one of the first things they want to do is wash it. Cleaning is often paramount on the mind of the owner because it is old, and because of that, the owner thinks that it must need cleaning. The very first question I usually am asked is, "How do I clean it?" The garment might be slightly yellowed due to age, and the owner might be concerned with how to get it to look fresh and clean.

I explain that care needs to be taken with any cleaning process, due to a number of factors, including such things as age, fabric content, construction, and so on. I might suggest having the item cleaned by a museum professional. However, if they are determined to try to clean it themselves, I might suggest that they give it a very gentle rinse in purified distilled water to freshen it, if it is colorfast and not too fragile. This sometimes is met with frustration, meaning the owner needs to be told again in more detail why the garment might not withstand conventional methods.

Aged textiles made from natural plant fibers (such as cotton and linen) and those of animal protein fibers (such as wool and silk) often behave quite differently from many of today's natural fiber fabrics, synthetics, and blends. They can have very different reactions to cleaning, storage, and so forth. We enjoy present-day clothing made of natural fiber fabrics, but even their care needs attention. We are lucky that we have care instructions for today's garments, and those who do not pay attention to them and wash a wool or cashmere sweater without following proper cleaning procedures might be very upset when the sweater is much smaller and no longer wearable.

An aged object might have a very faint brownish tint due to long exposure over the years to the air or packing materials around it. That patina, as it were, is not soil but an acidic reaction occurring due to age. However, to the unknowing owner, it might look like the textile is yellowed because it is soiled and needs laundering. The owner might think it isn't nearly white enough and want to bleach it, press it with a regular iron setting, or sometimes even put spray starch on it to make it look "crisp and new!" The results can be disastrous, especially if the garment or other textile is ruined.

Even if the object happens to look delicate enough to require some careful handling, one should understand that it is more than delicate; its age needs to also be considered. It may be even more fragile than it appears to be and need extra-special treatment. One needs to take into account all the materials it is composed of. For example, it may have decorative findings or trimmings on it that need to be examined closely, for they may also require special handling. There may be fugitive dyes present in some or all the colors in the fabrics. Substances left from past treatments involving cleaning solutions might cause reactions, and there may be residue from such things as tobacco smoke that permeated a storage container.

Please remember that all of this is being discussed to give you some idea of what might be involved in some circumstances, and it is not intended to be a recommendation. If you decide to experiment on a fragile object after careful examination, that is entirely your own decision. Also, be aware that a cleaning process may have very little or no effect on removing particular stains; that because of their very nature, they might not react to any cleaning method.

Next I want to discuss some procedures I have used that I consider important, to help you understand a little more about care. When I begin work involving an aged textile, the first step I usually take is to cover the examination surface securely with a clean sheet. I like to photograph everything before working on objects, and I also like to make notes on the condition before treatment of any type.

The next step is usually to prepare the object for a gentle vacuuming, only if it is strong enough. If it is very fragile, I do not attempt to vacuum it. Sometimes a soft brush may be used to remove dust, animal dander, insects, lint, or whatever else is present of that nature. If it is to be vacuumed, I use a very low-suction vacuum cleaner (handheld type usually, or a canister with a low suction adjustment) and a piece of coated screening. The screening is also bound on all edges with bias tape to protect the textile and is placed between the textile and the vacuum to protect the textile while vacuuming. Often this procedure is all that I need to do, as quilts and many other textiles often respond well to this process.

Next, if I feel it really necessary, I may decide to wet clean a textile. But if I do, I make sure I am well-prepared and have tested all parts of the object (trims, dyes, etc.) first to be sure it can handle it. Occasionally there are fugitive dyes that can be released if the textile is immersed in water, and it is important to always test the colors ahead of time. Using a cotton swab moistened with distilled water to gently but thoroughly blot the individual colors on a safe surface is a good test to be sure any dyes present won't run.

Before taking a chance to work on something, I always think about what I am doing very carefully. If it is a plain color and would take well to just a gentle soak in distilled water to remove light soil, I might decide that is the best treatment to use for freshening it up. One also needs to remember to be patient. After all, as mentioned, sometimes leaving it alone and just giving it extra gentle care may be enough.

When I do decide to wet clean a textile, I might begin by giving it a shallow soak in a large tray made for this type of treatment, and if such a tray is not available, I find that a clean bathtub works as well (and I always use distilled water). Be sure to remember that water has weight. That is important. The object is old and may be frail and should not be placed in deep water, only very shallow water with just enough to cover it. Sometimes I find that a screen beneath the textile helps to safely support the object in the water, and can serve as a protective measure to help when I slowly lift the object out of the tub.

If there is heavy soil, I might consider a soak with a mild surfactant (detergent). I usually do not agitate the object, although I might gently move the object slowly up and down a few times if necessary, to help the surfactant work better (usually on a coated screen), but only if I feel it is really necessary. If you decide to wet clean a textile, you might want to research surfactants online first, to see what museum professionals recommend.

Always keep in mind that if you are going to attempt to wet clean your textile, and that is entirely your decision, whatever goes in must come out, so you probably want to use only a small amount of mild detergent. I might do a test and select a small portion of a stain I want to remove. I might swab it with a surfactant using a Q-tip while holding the section of the textile being tested over a small dish and time it to see what results I get.

Also, I have found that doing the test on a similar piece of an aged garment or textile, or maybe a piece of the actual one if it has a section that won't be visible or needed later, is sometimes helpful. That way I can see how it reacts before I decide how to treat the actual object.

When ready, I carefully rinse the test area several times with clean distilled water, being sure to remove the detergent. Next, I sponge it very gently between layers of absorbent, clean toweling before laying it out carefully on clean sheeting or a flat drying rack (with a protected screen surface) to be air dried.

I have used several small dishwashing-type tubs at times when wet cleaning small textile objects, such as samplers, that have first been thoroughly tested for fugitive dyes or anything else that might cause a problem. It depends on the size of the object. That way I can gently and easily move them from the soaking water into clean water. I also use a gentle spray when deemed necessary to rinse a large textile in a clean tub as it drains between rinses, providing the process won't harm it.

If the object I am wet cleaning is very large, such as a quilt or carpet, I might find it necessary to make a very large container out of heavy-duty plastic, because a bathtub would not be big enough to do the job right. When doing that, a floor often is the best surface to place it on. While I was on sabbatical in Hawaii, I taught the faculty how to build a wet cleaning container. We used two-by-four sections of lumber and heavyweight, waterproof plastic sheeting, and when it was completed, I presented a demonstration to show students how to use it to wet clean a large object. Some curators use these. Different sizes can easily be constructed, and depending on the object, it is usually not very expensive, and parts are easy to store.

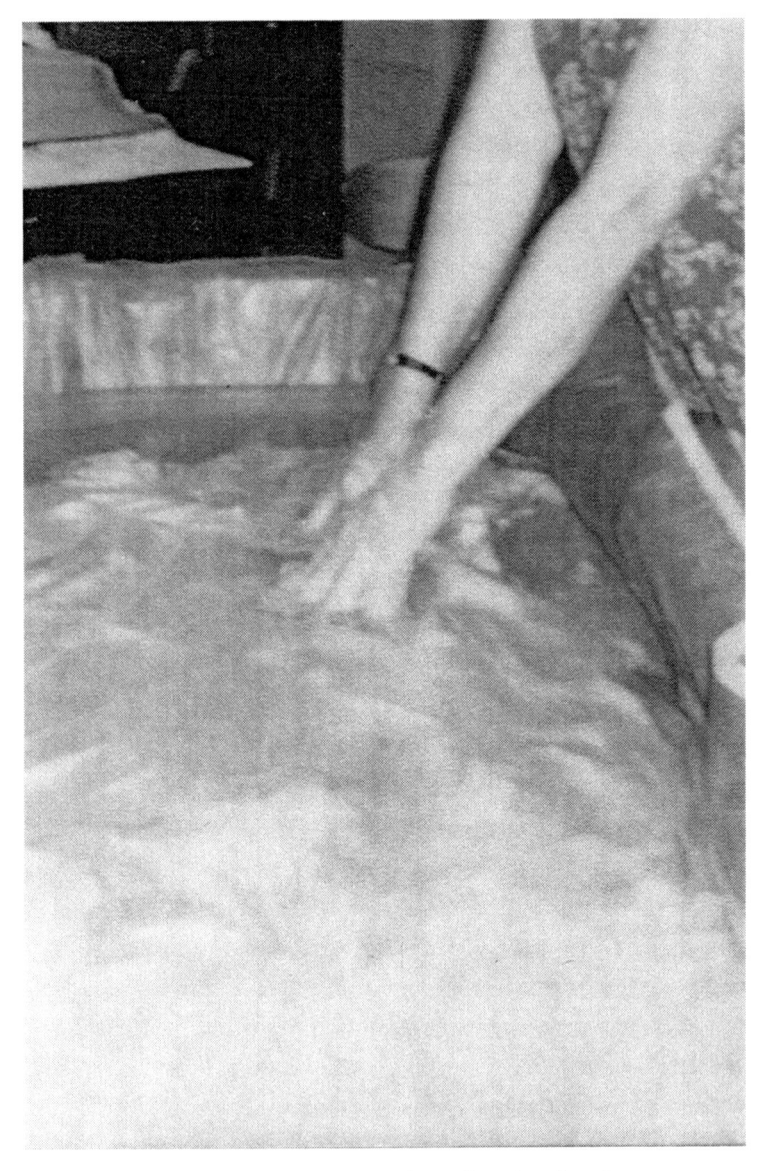

Figure 12. Wet cleaning a large, aged textile in handmade container.

When a smaller textile is almost dry, if I notice there are some wrinkles in it, a gentle finger pressing might help relieve them, but only if the fabric is not too frail. It really depends on how strong the garment, quilt, or any other textile object is, if the dyes are permanent, and what the general condition of the object is, how much work I will want to attempt.

Note that if you do attempt to utilize any wet cleaning methods, if all stains are not removed (sometimes the result), it frequently means they have become chemically permanent due to age and storage conditions, or they may have even been of a permanent nature originally. Again, seek professional advice on treatment before attempting any of this.

Chapter 8

The Shawl and the Piano

It was early summer, and I was driving to Maine with a friend to visit others for the weekend. We had decided to look for some antique shops on the way, as we had heard Maine had lots of them. Being a collector of sorts, my friend was quite excited about the adventure. Antique shops have always been of interest to me as well, not just because I like all kinds of antiques but because it also gives me a chance to talk to the dealers. Many of them are anxious to show their wares, and I enjoy having conversations with them.

I had not been in the habit of purchasing antiques myself in the past. However, now that I had a different occupation, I was thinking that maybe this could become a new hobby. My friend and I drove for hours and hours, catching up on everything, and after stopping for lunch about halfway to our destination, we managed to find a few out-of-the-way places to visit and look at furniture, jewelry, ceramics, paintings, and all sorts of things.

It was fun checking out the different shops, but it wasn't until we found a beautiful old barn by the side of the road that had a large hand-painted sign that said Antiques and some colorful drawings on the side of the building that it became more interesting to me. It was cheerful and different, and so we stopped to see what they had. There was a lot on display, and one particular object commanded my attention as I surveyed the large room. It was a beautiful, woolen, paisley shawl, and it was hanging up on the wall, suspended by two coat hangers. At first my instincts were telling me to talk to the dealer to get him to take down the shawl from where it was probably gathering dust, insects, and other things. As long as I was going to do that, why not look at the shawl more closely?

When I was the curator at the university, there were many shawls in that collection. They had been given by numerous donors over the years and took up a good-sized closet. There were several types of shawls. Paisley shawls from the United Kingdom and Kashmir shawls from India were highly valued. At one time, these large shawls were very popular in America and were included in many a lady's wardrobe. Some of these shawls still survive as decorative accessories or as art objects in homes today. But I never personally wanted to have one, until now. I liked this lovely, brightly colored shawl, and I was curious about it.

The young dealer was very friendly and not busy at the moment, so we had a chance to chat. He told me that particular shawl had belonged to a famous singer from the 1920s and 1930s. She was his elderly aunt, and he said that he remembered as a child how it used to be draped over the large grand piano in her home whenever he visited her with his parents. He told me all about her and how beautiful and talented she was. Being fond of singing myself, I really enjoyed hearing his story. I jotted down a few notes, and before I knew it, I was the proud new owner of that beautiful paisley shawl. I also was very happy to have rescued it from the barn wall.

The dealer and I chatted for a few minutes more, and I shared some earlier history with him, explaining how paisley shawls were actually a fashion accessory in many a fine lady's wardrobe, often worn over a full-skirted dress in the mid–late nineteenth century. The shawls were decorative, rather costly, and very popular. I told him there had been other more narrow shawls popular in the early nineteenth century, which had borders with similar designs, but they were not as large and usually rectangular in shape and of various lengths. I also told him how they were often worn with the semisheer, more columnar-shaped dresses and gowns of that (Empire) period, and how French Empress Josephine promoted the fashion, wearing a very long, narrow, rectangular shawl for her wedding in the early nineteenth century. He told me that he found it all quite interesting that shawls like the one I just purchased were not just for draping furniture but for people as well.

We have talked about handling aged textiles and related objects in previous chapters. Now I want to discuss some other situations that involve them and their various uses. In my work, antique dealers have occasionally approached me. They sometimes have questions regarding how they can better display and care for the old textiles and clothing items for sale in their shops. Some dealers know very little about what they have, including how fragile the items are and how to display them properly, and so they welcome some advice.

When I walk into an antique shop that has vintage clothing for sale, often an old garment will be on a hanger or a rack somewhere in a shop. Or it might be in a store window for prospective customers to view. It could also be in a box with other items for people to rummage through or in a lighted display case. In each location mentioned, there are things to be considered for the safety and care of this merchandise that is for sale.

Remember that a seller of such objects may not be versed in the care of aged textiles or clothing or even aware that special care is advisable when handling such merchandise. The specific techniques and the skills used by professionals in the field to care for aged textiles are not always known to them, and the information is not always readily available. Therefore, the seller may have only limited knowledge or no source information at all to share with a customer. The prospective buyer of vintage clothing may very well have questions for the salesperson about the garment or other textile object they may be considering to purchase. For example, a question may be, "If I buy it, how do I clean it?" Another may be, "How old is it and can I wear it?" It would be helpful and profitable for the dealer to have more information, and it is more impressive if the salesperson can share it with a customer.

Of course it should be noted that someone might already own a piece of vintage clothing, a historic garment, or another textile item. But whether it is merchandise to be sold or already owned, it might be subject to many of the same questions. It is important for one to be made aware of the various treatment possibilities. We will discuss this next.

The shop owner, small museum, historical society, and the individual collector may all have antique garments or other textiles of some age to deal with, and none of them should be forgotten. I have been asked questions by quite a few of them. They often ask for my advice or for information that can help them when displaying their textile objects.

I explain to them that aged garments, for example, might be very fragile and subject to damage quite easily if not handled carefully, and because of that, one needs to use caution when deciding how an object is to be displayed. If it is in a shop, how it is handled or put on display can result in profit or loss for a seller. It may also determine how the person who purchases it will be able to use it. It can also have an effect on the historic value of the artifact. Protecting the object from damage is important.

Therefore, when preparing to offer a vintage garment for sale, or when deciding if it is to be put on public display, there are a number of questions that need to be addressed. For example, should the item be placed in a store window? Think about this for a moment. Is it okay for the item to be safely displayed in a window or anywhere else where there is direct sunlight, artificial lighting, or ever-changing temperatures? When we go outdoors, we are told to put on protective clothing or creams to keep us from getting too much of the sun's harmful rays. If sunlight can cause damage to us, wouldn't it also be damaging to an old textile object?

Figure 13. Quilts displayed outdoors, in danger of fading.

Any strong light source, including artificial lighting in a shop, might eventually cause some damage. Perhaps there might be a fading of colors in a fragile textile and even a weakening of the textile fibers, which might dry out more over time in such conditions. There are protective methods professionals use to shield windows where light might enter, such as protective, low-light sources and specially treated glass. Some are expensive, and others not. Therefore, one may want to do a little research online to see what works best with his or her budget.

Of course, it is good if aged textiles can be kept out of direct light and be displayed with some filtered, low illumination. I would try to not let them be exposed too long when it is not necessary and remember to consider the age and condition of the objects.

If the shop is very bright, I might suggest making a special protective covering to drape over a gown or other merchandise that is especially delicate, and it could then be uncovered when needed for a customer. (Note that the cover should be able to keep out strong light but not be too heavy.)

There are other questions to be discussed, such as: should it be displayed flat or in a box, on a hanger, or on a dress form? Also, one might ask if it would help to have specific information on a label of sorts, for more appeal to a prospective customer. These are some of the subjects we can continue to discuss in the following chapters.

It is important to have some idea of how to protect the aged garments and textiles that will be on display so that they do not suffer major damage from their surroundings. Also, limiting the amount of handling they can undergo by clerks and prospective customers can be crucial to the survival of these objects from the past. It makes it more desirable to a purchaser when one sees careful display; it signifies that the store is helping to protect the condition and value of the objects.

Knowing something about the history and scarcity of the piece can also be useful to shopkeepers, helping them determine a reasonable selling price. Additionally, it makes the merchandise more desirable to a purchaser when one can secure some good information on the piece. Remember that it might be especially helpful for the dealer if he or she has some knowledge about the piece, such as age, fabric content, and previous use. That signifies that the shop really appreciates the customers' need for information.

Occasionally, qualified dealers do appraisals, and that is important to some customers. Small museums, historical societies, and collectors may also want their collections valued for insurance purposes.

Our search for knowledge continually helps us to keep up to date. I believe that when we have a better idea of what our treasures are and what we can do to take good care of them, everyone involved prospers in one way or another.

Chapter 9

Arms and Legs

It was early June, and I was a costume curator for a local historical society. The director had called that morning and asked me to meet with him at his office to discuss my plans for an exhibition I would be presenting that summer. It was going to be a mid-eighteenth-century wedding display. It would include a number of costumed forms in original garments worn in that period by a bride, groom, and attendants. I was really quite excited about it. While discussing my installation with the director, I expressed the need for suitable dress forms or mannequins for the historic clothing that I would be displaying in the exhibition. The problem I knew was trying to fit the expense into the budget, often a concern with small museums and historical societies. He told me that he would see what he could do. A few days later, he called me back to discuss setting up a time to meet.

When I arrived for the meeting, the director happily greeted me, telling me that he had some wonderful news. A very good friend of his who owned a department store was giving the society a gift! He was going to provide them with his used display equipment because he was purchasing new pieces for his store. The director had arranged for us to meet with his friend that morning to go to his warehouse, and I was relieved that we would be acquiring some display equipment, used or not. A short while later, we met the owner, and the three of us drove to the warehouse where the old mannequins were being stored.

When we got there, we parked the van and walked into the cavernous building. I looked around the large, open area, and it was almost frightening to see what was in front of me. There were many huge, wooden crates filled with all shapes and sizes of mannequin parts. There were heads in some of the crates and torsos in a few and lots of hands, arms, and legs in others. As I walked around the warehouse and examined the contents of the containers, I noticed that there weren't any numbers or markings on any of the numerous body parts to show which ones belonged together. I knew it was going to be a real challenge to find matching pieces when I started sorting through everything to find what I needed. Meanwhile, the two older gentlemen were standing nearby and smiling graciously. They seemed quite pleased with themselves, so I expressed joy as best I could while they looked on, having happily invited me to "help myself."

Of course the prospect of sorting through the crates was almost overwhelming, but I told myself it was important, and I began the time-consuming process. A few hours later, when I thought I had enough pieces that would match up and look like they belonged together somehow, the gentlemen helped me load them into the van. With legs and arms and other body parts stacked carefully, we began the trip back to the museum where I would be doing the installation the following week. Looking out of a window on the way back, I did happen to notice that more than just a few people were staring at us. I guess it must have been quite a shock to see all the legs and arms through the windows of the van!

The director, of course, was grateful to have the mannequins donated and happy that I could use them for my work. Although I was pleased to have the equipment, I was still worried about how I was going to be able to assemble the pieces I had chosen and have them fit together properly. I was hopeful that I could correctly assemble enough forms and that they would look good in the installation. And they did.

I want to share with you the following information on display, for I have often found it to be useful in my work with others. I shall discuss in more detail different methods that deal with displaying vintage clothing in shops, small museums, and historical societies. Hopefully these suggestions will be of value to you in caring for your textile objects.

In each situation I mention, there are things I consider for safety of items on display. Much of this information I would apply especially to small museum and historical society collections, and some of this I have found to also be helpful for dealers.

There is much to consider when displaying aged textiles and other related objects. For example, remember from our discussions that if a location one is considering for display has sun shining in on it through a window or other strong lighting sources from somewhere in the room, that could be harmful to an aged object. It would not be a suitable display area. I have frequently seen windows open in historic houses and in some reenactment villages where textiles and other aged objects are displayed. It may be a scene of sorts, showing an aged dress or other garment or textile item draped on a bed. The attempt has been made to make the object look like it has just been put there and will be used by a member of the family shortly. Bright sunshine is pouring in through the window, and everything seems to be giving the room a cheery appearance. Of course it certainly does look nice and inviting, but if the textile is old, it is being damaged in the process.

I have often suggested that in such a setting, staff make reproductions for display and keep the original objects in storage. At the same time, be sure that information is available to viewers so they know they are viewing reproductions, with the originals available for research purposes. That way, one would have an interesting representation without damage to the original artifact. In addition to the damage caused by sun shining into a room through an open window, remember that an open window can also admit all types of insects and other things that one does not want coming into a building. It is important to keep artifacts as protected as possible from foreign substances.

Air quality is something else one may need to consider when displaying aged objects. This is often important if there are fumes of any sort nearby, such as from cigarette smoke, food, or vehicle emissions. This might be a problem especially when objects are displayed in antique shops located on busy streets. Placing displays away from areas that could present possible problems helps protect them, and it is always best to secure a healthy environment for aged objects being displayed.

People often ask me specific questions concerning display of aged clothing. I explain that sometimes it depends on where one is planning to put an object. Some want to display objects on a flat surface to be viewed, such as in a museum case or on a shelf in a shop. It is usually a small garment, such as a bodice, shirt, baby dress, or christening gown. Perhaps it might even be a hat, purse, or some other type of accessory. Whatever it is, it needs to have a smooth surface underneath it, covered with clean fabric. Also, when placing an object on a protected surface, I might decide to have the covering underneath a contrasting color for accent. This works well particularly if the displayed object is sheer, such as a piece of embroidered lace, for it helps one to be able to see the design more clearly. A contrasting ground cloth can help to accent a full-size costume on display as well.

Figure 14. Restored theater costume on exhibit,
2006, Newport, Rhode Island.

Figure 15. Historic holoku on exhibit, 1994, University of Hawaii at Manoa, Oahu, Hawaii.

Sometimes a slanted board (I make sure it is painted to seal the wood to protect the textile from acidic residue) may be suitable for display purposes, but only if the fabric is lightweight and the slant is minimal, because the pull of gravity might cause sagging. Covering the board with fabric can also help to anchor a display. Remember that if any pins are used to hold an object in place, one needs to be sure that they are rustproof and won't damage the fabric. Pinning or carefully tacking down areas with thread is another method, rather than using pins or some other fastener, to protect a garment that needs to be attached to a display foundation. It depends on how fragile the object is. Sometimes using a lightweight, covered hanger or another method of support will help hold the garment in place as well and can be used so that pins or tacking are not needed. Of course, there are various ways to display vintage clothing. Hanger types can be used as well as dress forms and full-sized mannequins, and these are possibilities I shall discuss.

Often a garment will be stored in a closet on a hanger in a home or small museum collection or shop. The hanger may be a wire hanger or a wooden hanger. It may even be a wire hanger covered with foam, or a paper or plastic cover from a store, or even from a garment that has been professionally cleaned. Lightweight vinyl or plastic covers help keep garments separated in commercial situations and are used by some businesses but are not meant to be permanent coverings. These types of hangers and coverings are useful for handling new garments, and people may want to keep them with their garments for a short period, but if the cover looks like it is reacting in any way with the garment or is deteriorating due to the aging process, it needs to be replaced.

If one wants to protect or keep a garment for future use or display, it is important to consider a more protective type of cover for longtime storage. The garment can be better supported on a padded hanger that is covered with a fabric shield especially designed for the needs of a particular garment. Keep in mind that placing some non-textile-type materials next to a textile may actually cause a chemical reaction that might affect the textile. For example, an unpainted (unsealed) wooden hanger over a period of time might cause staining and deterioration to the object placed next to it or on it, which may result in damage to the object (because of the acidic residue in the wood). Protecting hangers with casings or coverings made of plain cotton muslin or cotton polyester blends helps to protect the textile by providing a barrier, helping to keep unsuitable materials nearby from damaging the garment that you want to protect.

There are many ways to design a hanger cover, but one of the easiest and quickest ways is to trace the hanger to be used on heavy paper and then add about three-fourths of an inch or so all the way around for a seam allowance (or more if pinking). Of course before constructing the cover from the paper pattern piece, you first want to be sure the fabric has been washed in a mild detergent with no perfumes or other additives, so that it is preshrunk. When dry, press the fabric smooth and then cut out your pattern pieces. (Pinking the edges gives a nice seam finish.) Once you have sewn your cover, turn it right side out and press it once more before using it.

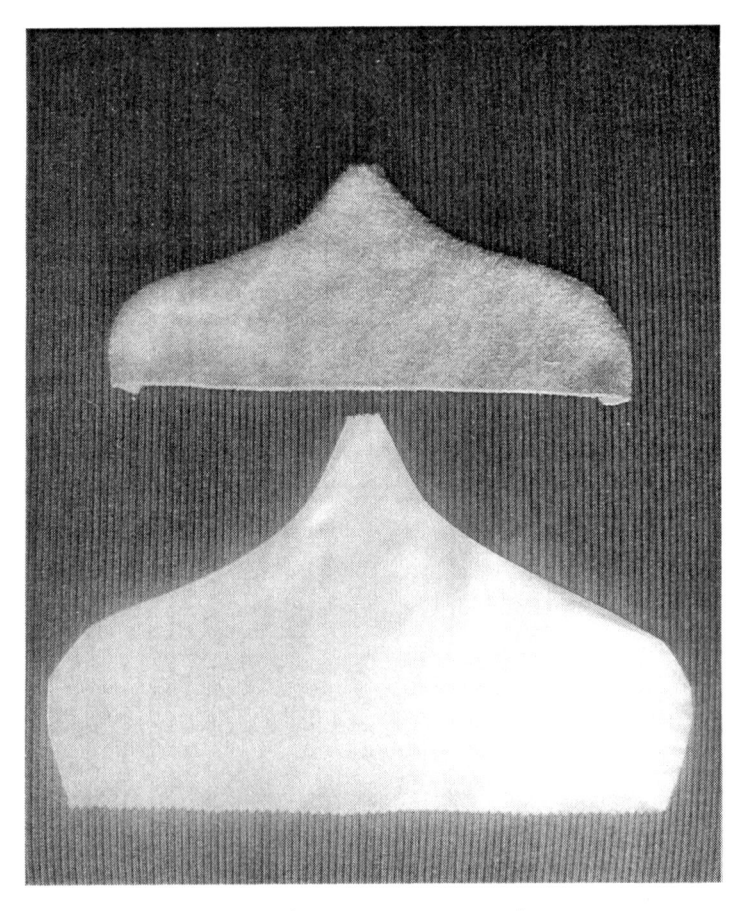

Figure 16. Hanger cover examples.

In addition to the plain fabrics mentioned, one also might consider a design for a stuffed hanger and covering using prequilted, plain fabric yardage that is used for making such items as mattress and table covers, found in fabric stores. Because the three-layer fabric usually is already quilted with a stuffing layer of polyester fiber or another type of filling, it has the cushioning you might desire for heavier garments. It is more convenient than having to add more stuffing separately. However, for more sculptured garments, even more shaping may be needed. If so, I would probably make custom, hand-stuffed hangers for them. Sometimes I use a wire hanger I can bend into shape for the foundation, depending on the particular garment. Padding does take time, but I find that it is worth it for very special costume pieces.

For lightweight garments, I might choose a quilted fabric that can be used under a plain, cotton cover on a regular, painted wire hanger. If a wooden hanger is being used for a heavy jacket or suit, the cover might have more quilted fabric layered underneath for a heavy garment, with a cover sewn over that stuffed material. I also might want a little heavier weight fabric for it than a regular hanger cover. If a garment is very heavy, I find that a firmly padded and covered wooden hanger works well. When any hanger is used to display a garment, the hanger should always be properly sealed, padded, and covered, to protect the garment.

Remember also that for unusually shaped shoulders from different periods, a handmade, stuffed wire hanger might work fine if you want to attempt it. As mentioned, I have experimented and constructed padded hangers for some period garments. I bend a wire hanger into the shape I need, pad and stitch it by hand, and then cover it tightly to keep the stuffing in place. Take note that there are also some commercial hangers that have a well-shaped design for some garments.

I always suggest that before one chooses a hanger type, one needs to examine the garment closely. The garment needs to be looked at particularly for voids, tears, and any other type of damage. Also notice if there are any buttons, heavy trims, or other attachments. If there is a large cloth flower or some such object pinned to the garment, of course it will need to be examined. Pins holding objects might be rusted, and the trim partially detached. There might also be loose trims or buttons that need stabilizing first. Look for tears and holes near them. There may be heavy folds in some garments that result in new stress being put on the garment. This is especially true if it is hung up (or displayed upright) without additional treatment or padding to give it the proper silhouette. Then again, you may find that the garment is just too cumbersome to be hung upright at all.

When a garment has parts that are awkward, heavy, loose, or very frail, that garment may not be a good candidate for hanger display. If it is fragile and being kept for research and just being stored and not on display, I find that boxed storage is safer. Then again, if it must be displayed, it may require more substantial support and need to be put on a dress form or mannequin. Some shops that deal in antique or vintage clothing a lot and some small museums might have these in stock.

But even a mannequin or dress form can stress an old garment if not properly handled. That can be a problem if it is the wrong size or shape for the garment or has removable parts that would be difficult to work with while one is dressing the form. If the garment is very fragile, it could be damaged if handled too much or forced to fit the form. (Note that what we are discussing in this chapter regarding shops selling vintage clothing also relates to small museum collections and historical societies with aged clothing and textile objects, the difference being that these objects are not for sale.)

Some shops selling vintage clothing to the public and some small museum collections and historical societies have little money to spend on expensive display equipment and find they have to take shortcuts. Because of that, many of the older dress forms that people use to display garments in a shop are secondhand. They may have been adjustable when originally purchased but now are partially deteriorated or have been overworked to the point that parts don't mesh the way they did originally.

There may be rough or sharp edges on a form that could damage a garment. If you plan to use a dress form, make sure it is suitable and examine it very carefully before using it. Also, if it is an old dress form with some damage, be very sure that you make some notes to that effect, writing down wherever you see that the dress form has spaces, sharp edges, uneven parts, faulty fasteners, etc. Once that is done, I always repair what needs attention in the best way I can and make sure there are no sharp edges. To my surprise, some people have even used duct tape to keep their form together if most of the fastening parts are missing. Not recommended of course, but this solution is one they probably used because it was absolutely necessary and nothing else was available.

I make sure to cover the dress form if need be, and if there is a soiled cover on a form, it needs to be removed—or re-covered if it is part of the body of the form and can't be removed—to protect the garment. Plain, clean cotton/polyester muslin yardage or sheeting that has been well washed and ironed is useful for covering old dress forms. Others have used stretch nylon, jersey fabric, or even pantyhose to cover forms as well.

For more lifelike clothing displays, we find there are many new innovations in mannequins today, and if the shopkeeper and others displaying aged vintage fashion can afford to purchase new period forms, that is always best, but they are often quite costly. Some period forms are molded and do not always require separate covers, but when they are covered with soft fabric first (and perhaps a petticoat or slip from the same period as the fashions and the mannequins), that often helps the garment to fit and drape better.

Frequently, as fashions change, secondhand forms become available from department stores when they are getting new ones, and you may be able to purchase some inexpensively from them or get a donation. They may not be exactly what you want, so pay attention to the silhouette to be sure you will be able to use them to display your aged garments properly.

Now I will discuss how I dress a mannequin. Please understand that I have been doing this for a long time and that experience certainly helps. If you have never put a garment on a mannequin, it may seem awkward at first. One needs to try to be as gentle with the garment as possible and make sure to measure everything first to be sure the fabric won't be stressed in the process. I find it important to examine the form carefully and think about how to begin and then just try to take it slowly. I recommend practicing with a present-day garment first, to get more familiar with the process.

When preparing to dress the mannequin, it is important to check all removable parts of the form before deciding to use it and to think about the order in which one needs to start the process. This is very, very important if a sleeve on the garment needs to be put on separately before attaching it to the form to fit the shape of the unattached arm of the form if that arm is bent. This could also apply when attaching a leg part for trousers, for example. Note that a dress or jacket may look like it will fit a present-day form, but remember attention needs to be paid to the silhouette, especially where shoulders and arms may be curved or too narrow or too broad for the garment to fit properly without stressing the fabric.

Again, don't forget that different periods in fashion often have different silhouettes, and you always need to check shapes and measurements carefully, to be sure a garment will fit correctly before attempting to put it on any display form, whether the form is period or modern day.

When putting a garment or an accessory on a form, it should look like it would on a person, and so I find that stuffing materials for garments on display is often necessary, and if there is not enough proper support underneath the garment, I often use acid-free tissue. With clean hands, I like to gently scrunch or mold the tissue and then place it where needed to help shape the silhouette. Sleeves that need fullness are good candidates for this. If there are wrinkles that need relaxing, layering smooth layers of tissue over the scrunched tissue can provide additional support. This is also a good treatment for full skirts. Also, always try to remember not to put too much tissue under the garment or other object, to avoid stressing it.

If one wants to be sure that the stuffing is lightweight and fluffy, another type of stuffing material one might like to use is polyester fiber filling (like the kind often used to stuff new pillows). It will give a different effect than tissue, and I do find it is not usually as successful at holding a shape in some situations, so one must experiment at times.

Remember that one must always use care when inserting any stuffing material into a garment that might need support. When sleeves are supposed to be puffed or rounded, or if they are long and narrow, it is important to not have jewelry on that could snag a fabric, and always have very clean hands or thin cotton gloves on when handling old textile items. (No lotions or perfumes.)

I have used other stuffing materials, depending on the situation. For example, a soft piece of muslin or a piece of soft velvet under a lightweight textile fabric or a piece of lace might give soft support to a crease or help with sagging in delicate areas. Just be sure that whatever you plan to use is not going to cause any damage to the textile.

One more note for dealers, museums, and historic societies I want to mention is that providing a printed description and information about the object along with dates is often helpful and appreciated by the viewer. You may even want to have a printed sign attractively done requesting that viewers not touch the item. I like the label to be polite but firm. "Thank You for Not Touching" or a sign that says something like "Handling Hastens Deterioration" are favorites of mine. A sign in an antique or vintage clothing shop saying to ask for assistance is also good practice.

Chapter 10

Lessons to Learn

I heard the phone ringing. I answered it, and a friend was on the other end inviting me to an opening at the local historical society. He was on their board and said that it was to be a very grand affair. He was excited and wanted me to see what the institution had just put on exhibit. He also told me that a notable longtime member and wealthy benefactor of the society had actually designed the exhibit, and a gown that had belonged to one of her ancestors was the focal point. Of course I would attend.

The afternoon of the opening arrived, and my friend asked me if I could meet him right away ahead of other invited guests so that he could give me a private showing. I was anxious to see what all the fuss was about and met him at the entrance. We walked into the building, and straight ahead of us was the exhibit. It depicted an eighteenth-century room with furniture of the period and a mannequin dressed in an eighteenth-century gown of silk brocade.

The garment was on display in the center of the room, and from a distance I thought that the way the gown's pastel shades of silk brocade glistened under the chandelier was quite nice, but then when I looked more closely at the gown, I was horrified to see that the gown had been put on the mannequin backward! I immediately told my friend, who then totally panicked. I asked him if there was enough time to fix it, even though it was probably much too late for that. I was also informed by an assistant that the woman who had designed the exhibit was not on the premises yet, and even if she was, she would be very upset, for she would certainly not like being told that she had made a mistake. Nevertheless, we frantically tried to find a solution, and we talked about ways we might be able to substitute it for something else until it could be redone, but there was not enough time to do anything before the opening, which was about to begin. Unfortunately, the gown had to be left the way it was for the time being.

Amazingly, I did not hear anyone make a comment about the gown being on backward during the opening that day, which for the woman's sake and the society was probably a really good thing. However, I must say that I saw to it that the exhibit was corrected a few days later, after she and they were all gently educated on women's eighteenth-century fashion.

Today, there are many individuals who enjoy learning about what people wore in the past, along with other memorabilia that has been collected. Just about every town in the country with a reasonable population has a building where there are collections of historic items that are on display for the public to view. Each one of these facilities has its own personality that is shaped by where it is and by the people who have lived there, along with what it contains and who manages it.

Small museums and historical societies often have an inventory of clothing and textiles and other objects that they like to put on display. However, some find that they don't have enough financial resources to have more than a few people employed, and they find the help they need by making use of volunteers when they are available. These volunteers may or may not have any knowledge of what the collections contain or how to handle them. Because it looks like fun and they think that it is interesting to work with historic items, they often volunteer in their spare time, and many institutions are grateful. Working together as a team, the small museum and its staff and volunteers need to learn how to care for their collections and how to display them properly for public view.

A small museum or historical society may be located in an old house near the center of town, having been left to the town to be used for a museum. Some may have a small budget, and others may even have a large endowment to help support their facility. I have found that many of these institutions contain wonderful articles of clothing and accessories that have been donated over the years by members of the community, with important historical ties to the original owners and the town. Donors who have inherited them want the items to be shared with others as part of the history of their community, and at the same time, they want them to have a "good home." They may also have some related information to share with the population, which might be valuable for research purposes.

This all needs to be protected and properly cared for. Unfortunately, some facilities are maintained by well-meaning people who are not trained in museum techniques, and because of that and lack of funding, objects are not always as well cared for as they could be. We have already discussed some of the cautions to be observed in caring for historic clothing and other textile objects in earlier chapters. Here we will discuss certain points that relate more to a small museum or historical society than an individual collector or dealer in antique textiles. These collections, unlike the articles found in a shop that has aged objects for sale, are primarily in existence more for long-term educational value and research rather than for private ownership by individuals.

The means of display is similar to what we have discussed previously, but storage and record keeping and preservation are additional concerns we can now explore. I have often thought that one could relate a collection of historic artifacts to a library, because like a library, everything needs to have a specific location and should be in as good condition as possible for public viewing and research purposes.

The objects always need to be readily available when requested, and that requires very good record-keeping practices.

For example, while a curator, one of the requirements of my position was to know where every artifact was at a moment's notice, and I was in charge of a collection that contained many thousands of objects. We are constantly advancing in this area and developing better retrieval methods all the time, but to really know your own collections well is always beneficial. I often stress that striving to gain extensive knowledge of a collection and its components, along with being well-organized, is beneficial, because without organization there can be chaos, as we all know.

I would like you to remember also that organization extends to new acquisitions as well, for most collections continue to expand as time marches on, and their history needs to be recorded for future generations. This all takes lots of time and effort. Once an object is accepted, I always see that it is acknowledged, usually in a thank-you letter to the donor, a copy of which is then placed in a separate donor file. Institutions may also want to consider getting appraisals in certain situations, depending on perceived value. This may be involved when one is in the process of making a determination regarding where the object will be kept and if extra protection is needed for it when on display and in its storage location.

Inventories can be handled using simple record-keeping procedures or a computerized system or both. For example, while curator at the university, at one point our collection was growing by leaps and bounds. More and more donations were continuing to be accepted, and I felt that it was time to seek some help. One day I made a decision to approach my dean to discuss new computer systems that were being developed at various institutions that I had read about. I set up a meeting with her and told her that I especially wanted to visit the Smithsonian Institution in Washington, DC, and told her why I was hoping that I would be able to make an appointment with them. She agreed wholeheartedly with my request and provided funding for my travel and stay in Washington, DC, for meetings and study with the museum staff.

Once I was at the Smithsonian Institution, their staff was very welcoming and helpful and spent time explaining the system, giving me a private tour of the facilities, and providing me with the information I needed. When I returned to the university, I applied for and secured a grant and began the steps necessary to start work on a computerization project for our collection. The dean was also extremely helpful in us obtaining new computers for the collection, and so began the new inventory procedure. As it progressed, graduate students were assigned to help me enter information from the original system, and as new items were donated, they were entered into the new database as well. This all took some time, but I felt that it was important because of the huge increase in our inventory.

However, the simpler inventory procedure that was in existence when I first started working at that university was actually very easy to deal with and quite efficient for a long time. I think it may be helpful to some small museums, historical societies, and maybe some theater groups to think about how it was set up, because it might help them in some way when they are dealing with their own collections, so I shall explain.

It consisted of two file cabinets containing an index-card file for donors and an index-card file for the inventory. The index-card file (inventory) cards were listed by category first, and each card under each category had sections listed by century and decade. The cards filed had the description of the particular object being accessioned written on the card and included donor name, address, date acquired, notes of a specific date or occasion if significant, along with the description and location of the object in code, on the back of the index card.

There was also a main file folder that listed all the categories in order, which remained with the files at all times and a complete donor file for the donor letters and any additional information of importance needed for research purposes. There also was a file containing all the location codes kept separately for safety. I found it all quite good and easy to use. I still think that this type of file system would be good for some small collections without any funding available for a computer system.

Now I want to talk about labeling. When an acquisition is accepted and acknowledged, it needs to be labeled. Over the years, many methods have been used, some good and some not. For example, it seems unbelievable to me, but at one time in the distant past many artifacts were marked with indelible ink. Back then, I guess this was thought to be a safe and permanent means of identification. It was used quite a lot, especially for hard objects, but sometimes on textiles as well. When I go to exhibitions, I always look extra closely at items on display, and believe it or not, occasionally I still see some objects marked that way! New ways of labeling have been developed over the years, but still one can find a few old labels remaining intact in some collections. Because textiles were sometimes marked with ink that way and the ink cannot be removed, it may be hidden when the object is on display, but that is not always possible, especially with fragments.

I have unfortunately seen artifacts with actual adhesive tape on them that is printed with ink and some where the tape is of fabric that is sewn on to the garment or other textile, or even stapled on, believe it or not. It is good to protect all of these objects, but sometimes incorrect and damaging procedures such as these mentioned can reduce value of an object if they cause damage, and they may also impair the beauty of it when on display.

When I first worked as a decorator before becoming a curator, it was always with new fabric, and labeling was not a problem, for these textiles were not museum pieces at the time. If saved over the years and donated later to a museum or society, they would then need labeling for identification of course. Today we know more about all of this, and there are constant improvements.

Common sense tells us to be careful when dealing with a museum piece, and how we do that can depend on different things. Garments in museum collections should not have dangling tags with long strings hanging from them in a closet, in my opinion. However, I have seen museum storage where that is in practice. One must think about this. When removing a dress from such a closet, to be protective of the object, one should be very careful, especially with dangling tags nearby, but not everyone is. They may be in a hurry or have other things distracting them at the time, and that can be dangerous. For example, if the garment is old and fragile, a sleeve can be caught on another tag, and one or both garments might be damaged in the process. You would think that common sense would say to be very careful, but people sometimes are not, and accidents can happen.

If one would like more visibility for identification, I find that a short string and small, acid-free tag is safer and not so much in danger of being caught on another garment nearby. However, if one was to remove the garment for study or display, the tag would still be visible, so it would need to be tucked inside the garment when being prepared for display. It also would probably not be labeled with complete information about the garment, that information being in the files, but it could be used to list the decade and the location code, which would help one with returning it later on to its proper storage location. Some like to use the hanger for the tag, which makes it easier to see the information, but the problem then is that often the garment is removed from the labeled hanger, and that information is lost.

The collection I worked with was originally labeled by several others long before I became the curator, but I found it quite suitable and very efficient at the time. The inventory tags with descriptions and location, which were about an inch each way in size and the shape of a regular tag, were sewn into the armcye (armhole area) of each garment. The reason was probably because the armhole of a garment is always present whether sleeveless or not, and a tag can be hidden easily if need be. All tags were sewn inside on the seam allowance and on the same side (left armcye) with the garment placed on the rack to the right side, the front facing out, making it the (left sleeve) side where the tag would be easily accessible when necessary. I made sure that all hangers always faced the same direction and kept everything in order, making it easy to see without having to remove the garment. I found no fault with the organization and continued that practice for some time, because it worked.

I also gave each closet a code letter or name and separated the sections by decades so that all garments were placed in chronological order on the storage racks. An inventory of each closet was posted on the inside of each storage unit for easy access as well for a quick overview of the closet contents.

Some facilities may use other methods of course. The one that I used with the collection I managed was both safe and functional. When I first became the university curator, the facility was fairly dated and had been moved several times from one end of the department to the other. It consisted mostly of large collections of laces, shawls, fans, shoes, undergarments, hats, etc. The strong point of that collection I considered to be wonderful eighteenth- and nineteenth-century garments that had belonged to the people of that area long ago. There was some good recorded local history in the files, which was of help to those people who came from near and far to do costume research.

When I had been there a few years, some quilters who wanted to see our quilt collection approached me. They were very pleased with the quilts I showed them, and then one of them asked me if I would ever be willing to do a quilt exhibition. I thought that would be great. I decided that if my dean and department chair said it would be okay, I would do it. It was fine with them and the start of a large project for me, for there was much to do.

In addition to my regular work, I was busy selecting quilts, finding space, setting up the event, and acquiring professional security for the exhibition, which would run one week on campus and be open to the public. There was some funding from the college, along with lots of help with building the display foundations donated by the theater department and their students on campus.

Quilters came to see the exhibit and to attend a special workshop on quilting given by an invited guest quilter of renown, and lots and lots of people from the community and elsewhere also viewed the exhibition. I kept records, and when it was over, it had averaged about 250 or more visitors a day. The dean allowed me to hire a professional photographer to photograph all the quilts in the collection so that there would be a permanent record of the exhibition quilts in the collection, and I also was able to design a commemorative poster along with the publications department at URI for the exhibition ("American Quilts, An Exhibition from the URI Collection Celebrating Rhode Island's 350th Anniversary"), and I did another smaller quilt exhibition at the Rhode Island State House for the governor of Rhode Island that year.

Figure 17. American quilts on exhibit, 1986, University of Rhode Island, Kingston, Rhode Island.

Later on, I worked on another grant, and when it was received, I was able to purchase more acid-free boxes along with rolling closet storage, which was installed in two rooms of the collection and contained metal shelving and sections for hanging garments, along with large storage cabinets suitable for flat textiles. The procedure for storage continued in the same manner, but now there was easier accessibility and visibility. Quilts were given a new home in the large, flat storage drawer cabinets purchased, with drawers big enough to spread out a quilt. Several quilts could be layered full size in the same drawer, which also made them more visible. They no longer needed to be folded up in boxes, which helped keep them relaxed.

Some small museums and historical societies and others may be able to get support for such equipment if they have people who can help them write grants. It is a time-consuming undertaking but well worth it if one is successful, and I always think it is worth trying whenever possible.

One of the first things I did when becoming a curator was to learn as much as I could about air quality and ultraviolet effect on aged textiles. The reason for that was that I had a large showroom in the collection. It contained display platforms and cases and mannequins, and it was my responsibility to do displays periodically for students, faculty, and public visitors to the collection as well as for several other locations on campus.

One side of the collection room was all windows, and I worried about light damage. I also worried about air quality because of the age of the building and because classrooms often had windows open to the weather that could bring outside air into the collection space when people entered it. I decided to approach my dean and department chair at the time, and with their help I was able to get ultraviolet filtering material for the windows and an electronic air filtering system for the collection display room, along with several air-conditioning units for the large storage rooms.

When it was affordable, because of the value of the collection, I also sought approval for a security system that I thought necessary to protect the collection, and that request was granted and installed by the university. Each morning and evening during the week, I called to notify the campus police when I entered the collection, and again when it was closed for the day, keeping everything safe under lock and key when school was not in session. Small museums, historical societies, and school collections may or may not have security systems. Those that don't may want to think about whether or not these measures might be worth considering, especially if their collections are of great value, and try to get funding if they feel it necessary.

Lighting is also important to consider. If you have a collection in a small building that has lots of light, today they have even more advanced materials for sun protection, and if you are doing displays, it is something you may want to investigate. Air conditioners are also pretty common, and many places have them, depending on affordability. I have been in small museum buildings on a sunny day when the windows are wide open, and insects, bright sunlight, lack of security, and more can be problematic. Common sense should tell us to close them if we have an exhibition in place. So much of all this is common sense, and if one can be vigilant and find help and funding, it is certainly important to try to protect your collections.

It has been a while since I was the curator of the university collection I have mentioned, and, at the time, a lot of what I did was fairly new (and I was pretty young and ambitious too). Today, of course, there are new advancements, and if you go online and visit well-established museum facilities, you can see some of what they do and get ideas for your own collection. I do hope some of what is shared here is helpful and will inspire you.

Now we will discuss storage. I have found that house museums and some historical society facilities are similar in how they are arranged storage-wise, especially if they are in houses that once belonged to people and are now owned by these organizations. Some have large rooms and large closets. Others have large rooms and no closets, because the original owners used armoires and trunks and hooks on the wall for their clothing and textiles. Both types have been converted, and storage has been built into the houses for the collections now stored there. Some still use furniture, such as armoires and trunks. Others use all these types of storage.

Any storage location needs to be carefully examined for nails, soil, unsealed acidic wood, and other surfaces that may cause damage to an artifact. Most curators are particular about what finishes and materials are next to aged textiles, because they know that they sometimes interact with the textiles and might cause damage over time. Insects are a concern, and keeping spaces as clean as possible using safe cleaning methods is important. In the beginning, I often used unbleached, well-washed muslin to line shelves and as a dust cover for items. Later, we had acid-free materials in most situations when affordable, although muslin is still good for many other purposes. If your facility can afford acid-free board and tissue, you may want to use it, depending on your budget. Storing small items in acid-free boxes on the shelves seems to be fine if the shelves are protected. Metal museum shelving units are specially made for this but costly, so improvisation sometimes is necessary.

It is expensive to renovate an old building and install such equipment. Of course it really depends on what the small house museum can afford and if the structure itself can support the weight. Some small historical societies, like some college collections, have different construction, and it may be easier and therefore less expensive to install regular storage units. All of this needs to be considered before making changes to collection storage areas.

In a small house museum, the kind of storage utilized often depends on where the emphasis on each collection lies. If there are a lot of flat textiles, they might be perfect candidates for armoires and trunks in good condition, which were actually built to hold such objects. If the collections have lots of clothing, hanging space may be needed, although small objects like hats, shoes, and wraps, properly packaged, may be stored better in furniture.

Small house museums from the eighteenth and early nineteenth centuries often have only small textile collections, and the bulk of their collections may be furniture of the period of the building. Here you may find that clothing in the inventory is stored in trunks and cabinets that are on display, and objects are brought out of storage only for special reasons. Don't forget to make note that these trunks need to be properly lined to protect textiles too.

Again, display needs to be thought through carefully. We have discussed display in the preceding chapter, but let us review a few major points. Sun can damage a textile and other aged objects. When one is on tour in some old historic house museums, one may notice sunlight shining through windows (closed or open) and directly on the textiles and other furnishings. Yes, it looks peaceful and makes one feel like the family is still there, giving a human touch we like, but the sunlight that is penetrating the objects eventually will cause damage to them. There are ways to coat the windows or curtain them if affordable, but if not, more sensible placement of objects away from the windows can help as well. Of course, we need to consider handling, display, and all the rest, but common sense is always recommended.

Unfortunately, many small historic house museums and historical societies are on a tight budget and may not be able to afford climate control and other protective devices for their collections. Therefore, seeking grant money is a worthwhile effort, especially when one succeeds.

Chapter 11

Show Biz

It was the end of the school year and time for me to think about what to do for the summer. I had heard that people were getting excited about a movie that was being made locally and were looking forward to seeing some famous film stars. The local newspaper had printed that extras would be needed for the film, and that was good news for those who fantasized about becoming famous on the big screen someday. One quiet afternoon, a couple of my colleagues stopped by my office to tell me they had just tried out to be extras for the upcoming film, but weren't the "right type." They said they thought I was, however, and they wanted me to go try out, right then. I had the summer vacation ahead of me and the time to do something different, and so, after thinking it over, I decided to take their advice and check it out.

When I got to the building where auditions were being held, there was a long line of people waiting to be interviewed. At first I thought maybe I wouldn't wait around, but after about twenty minutes or so standing in the line, I found myself engaged in a conversation with the friendly security guard standing nearby. We were chatting away for quite a while about various subjects as the line moved slowly along, and then he asked me what kind of work I did. I told him I was a curator of historic costume and textiles, and he wanted to know what that involved, and it was while I was telling him about my work that

I felt someone touch my shoulder from behind. The guard smiled as I turned and looked to see who it was. There was a woman standing there with an even broader smile on her face. "Hi, I heard some of what you said. Do you know a lot about historic costume?" she asked me. I said that it was part of my job and that I had to know as much as possible about the subject because I was a curator and managed a large collection. The woman appeared quite interested and seemed to be thinking intently about what I had said. Then she asked me if I might answer some questions for her. I told her that I was waiting to audition. "Don't worry about that. I will make sure you get your audition," she said. So I said it would be okay, wondering what it was that she wanted to ask me. She then told the security guard it was all right to let me out of the line because she was going to take me into the wardrobe room, which was close by but off-limits to the public. She evidently had some authority. He looked at her and nodded as he lifted the security rope, and then she and I left the hallway as I waved good-bye to the friendly security guard.

As my new friend and I walked, we talked a little while, and she introduced herself, giving me her name and her title. Then she guided me into a large room that was filled with costumes and many accessories for the upcoming film. I was happy to see all the clothing, especially some beautiful designer originals I noticed, which she then pointed out as being from a private collection in California.

There were also racks of men's suits and more of women's garments, and tables that were laden with beautiful beaded and sequined dresses, feather boas, headdresses of ribbon and sequins, beaded purses, hats, and shoes, all in the style of the 1920s. There were several assistants in the room who were working with the costumes, and I was introduced to everyone there. She showed me some of the special costumes made for the principal actors and told me who would be wearing certain ones in the film. I was intrigued with all of it and was becoming more and more interested and curious by the moment. I loved the fashions of the period and also the excitement of being in the company of these impressive Hollywood people. I sent a silent "thank you" to my two colleagues who had insisted that I go try out for the film.

As we walked around the room, she led me to one of the tables and asked if I would be willing to give her some information on the fashions and the period and help her to better coordinate some of the ladies' outfits. She was very confused about what pieces needed accessorizing and where and how. I explained a few things to her and the others and told them a little about the period and what were some of the most popular styles then. With her permission, I gently placed some of the garments and wraps together on the table to illustrate various combinations and ways the garments might have been worn originally.

Many of the dresses on loan from the private collection were originals and mostly French and would be worn by specific extras chosen for certain scenes. A well-known designer was creating the principal characters' costumes, and I was shown a few of those along with some of the designer's sketches that were nearby. The colors for each of them I noted were carefully coordinated and chosen to represent the personalities of the characters. For example, I noticed that the more gentle characters were being costumed in pastels, and the more outgoing in brighter colors. They were all very beautiful and well accessorized in the sketches.

While I was in the costume and wardrobe rooms, I looked at my watch, and almost an hour had gone by. I reminded my new friend that I was still there to try out for the movie, and she said okay, she would take me to see the casting people, which she did later on, and I was told by the casting director that I could be an extra if I wanted to be one. However, as the day wore on, I found that I was more interested in spending time with the wardrobe people. They seemed to appreciate me as I did them and said they were grateful for the information I was providing them. I was grateful for the exposure to the wonderful costumes, and I asked if I could be on the set helping out as a volunteer. I was told that of course I could, and so that was the beginning of my summer adventure.

I spent quite a bit of time with the costume and wardrobe people and also some of the movie crew during that summer. I went to lunch a few times in town with one of the actors who was a main character (!) and occasionally lunched with a few of the other actors and the crew as well, which was a lot of fun. I really felt right at home with them, maybe because it reminded me of how much I loved being in theater productions and helping out backstage when I was in college. I have been in a few films myself off and on as well, so I felt very comfortable with all of it.

Figure 18. Author in costume, 1997, on movie set.

Because I got to be involved to quite an extent with the film that summer, I was often on the set. One night in particular, I especially remember because that night was quite different, to put it mildly. The actors and the extras were doing one particular party scene over and over and over again. It was being filmed at a mansion during the wee hours of the morning, and everyone was working really hard, until it got so that some of the extras were getting a little silly because they were very tired, it being such a long night. Then, all of a sudden, somehow an extra was accidently knocked into the pool! There was major chaos, as one can imagine, because they were actually filming at that moment. Before anyone could stop what was happening, however, others were joining the extra in the pool, and now it seemed that almost everyone was in the pool—and of course they all were fully dressed for the scene! There was lots of confusion, and to make it even worse, many of the beautiful costumes they were wearing were being damaged.

The next day, I walked into the wardrobe room and saw that many of those garments were hanging on racks to dry, but one knew by looking at them that most were beyond saving. As I gazed around the room, I was in dismay, as were the wardrobe people, at the sight of what had been beautiful period garments, now only faded, shredded, and misshapen fragments. Of course "the show must go on," as the old saying goes, and soon everyone that had been in the pool had a new garment to wear. I think many felt badly for what had happened and now realized how fragile aged silks could be. It was quite a catastrophe but perhaps not a total waste, because I believe the filmmakers liked the scene so much they decided to keep it in the film!

When school was back in session and others found out about my experience with the film, there was quite a bit of interest, so I wrote an article about it, which was published by my university in the alumni magazine. I also managed to acquire some promotional materials from the movie company, and I donated them to the collection. When students found out about how I spent my summer and who I spent it with, they loved hearing about it and asking lots of questions. I think that some of them might even have been inspired to look for a career in film or theater someday.

Film companies and theater groups mostly need costumed actors in their productions. But sometimes they don't find the right information they need to costume their performers properly and make mistakes. This can be a problem if the film or play is a popular one, especially if people who have some knowledge of historic clothing attend it. When it is a professional film or play with a good budget, designers are usually hired to make sure everything is correct.

However, if an amateur production is being produced and has volunteers with little or no actual experience working with period clothing, they can make serious mistakes. This can happen if people are dressing their actors when they don't know how costumes should be worn. This might interfere with the story and can also make a production look unprofessional. Most people excuse such mistakes if noticed, when it is an amateur production, but it is always better to do the needed research and try to do a good job whenever possible.

Many colleges and small theater companies have costume or wardrobe rooms that contain donated clothing, with some pieces that are original period garments. Sometimes these garments are very interesting and may be very desirable to an actor who might want to wear one onstage. Unfortunately, when they are worn onstage, they don't always survive for another wearing. Because they are thought of as making great theater costumes, the actors and others may not realize how fragile these aged garments are and handle them improperly.

Tagging an original garment with a warning to handle it with care can help to protect it while in storage. When wearing it onstage, anything can happen, depending on the character's role, and that means the actor needs to be reminded it is fragile. Knowing how old a garment is and what period it comes from is a clue to how fragile it might be. For example, some early nineteenth-century garments may seem stronger when handled than some from the 1920s. This is because the earlier ones were made of sturdy cotton, linen, or silk that has probably aged fairly well, causing them to not look as old as they really are, but they are still old.

One must be observant and examine all aged garments carefully before deciding if they are going to be used, whether for theater, the movies, or just for a special occasion. For example, when handling sheer silks and crepes and satins of the 1920s, which are often beaded and therefore quite heavy, one needs to be especially careful. They are beautiful to look at but can become quite stressed when hung on a hanger or worn by a person. (Some are so heavy I think it is amazing that they were ever actually worn.) Remember that these dresses need to be carefully wrapped and stored in an acid-free box if possible (and gently nestled in acid-free tissue to prevent shifting when the box is moved) and never hung on a hanger. Theater or film companies who have actors dancing in these creations often find that many a beaded dress has ended up with lots of its trim on the floor while someone frantically tries to retrieve all the beads and crystals.

Keep in mind that the thread that garments were sewn with will weaken over time. Old seams may split quite easily with just a little pressure on them when one is handling or trying on an aged garment. There are of course other things to be wary of as well, such as rusted hooks and other sharp objects that may be in or on the garment. Always examine your aged garments carefully, inside and out.

When an aged garment is going to be worn onstage (or by an individual for a party or other function), it is most likely for a very special role, and it especially needs to be protected from coming apart on the person. Whenever I work with one, I make sure that it is lined and supported from the inside and create a separate liner that will be a little smaller than the garment, to fit the wearer who will be in the garment. This helps protect the garment and keeps seams from splitting as a result of movement. I will also give instructions on how to move in it. If the garment doesn't fit properly, but one still wants the look of it, I might make a copy of it in a person's size and keep the original as is.

When at the university, I was often visited by theater classes who sketched and measured original period clothing in our collection as part of a class assignment. Some costume designers may also measure the individual sections of an old period garment, do a sketch, and recreate it. This can be a great way to make an authentic-looking period costume, and one can still keep the original garment for future research and use if needed for other stage and period film productions.

Accessories, such as purses, hats, shoes, and so on, need to be the same period as the garments worn onstage to be convincing. And don't forget undergarments, which are quite important and need to be researched, for they often help provide the proper shape or silhouette and can be a crucial part of a period costume. I have seen some young celebrities dressed in expensive designer originals from much earlier periods, who seem to have no idea that they are not wearing the fashion correctly. It just doesn't present a nice appearance when the support structure is all wrong.

There are distinctive differences in period fashions. Many people like to watch period films not just for the story but also for the costumes worn, which help set the scene and make it more memorable. If you are making films or doing plays, remember to do research on that period so that you know what needs to be done to achieve the proper silhouette when you attempt to clothe your performers.

Also note that sometimes one may want to wear an aged garment for a wedding or some other function and not just onstage, and the same principles most likely apply. If you want to keep your treasure, do your research, protect it by handling it properly, and always try to use it in the best possible way you can.

Chapter 12

Treasures Found

People often come across clothing items and other textiles that have been packed away and forgotten, and on discovering them, they either toss them out, try to find a way to recycle them, or give them to someone else. They may end up in secondhand shops, antique shops, garage sales, theater collections, etc. Not knowing much about what the found objects are, some people will seek help and advice.

One day while I was at work, my secretary called to tell me that I had an unexpected visitor who wanted to visit the collection. She did not have an appointment, but I was not overly busy at the moment and had some time to spare, so I went down the hall to greet her. The woman was holding several large shopping bags. We introduced ourselves, and then she said that she wanted to show me what she had brought with her.

We went back to my office and placed the bags on an examining table in the next room. She told me that while cleaning out the basement in her newly purchased house, she had come across the bags of clothing in some old cardboard boxes. She didn't know anything about them or how long they had been there, or who they might have belonged to originally. Having no need for them, she wondered if I thought anything would be of use to the collection.

I opened the bags and examined the contents and saw that most of the clothing appeared to be from the 1940s and 1950s. They were obviously before her time and probably had been packed away years before, maybe to be used later on for something else, or maybe they were just forgotten. The young donor said I could do as I wished with them, and she left, glad to have found a place for them.

The next day, I examined what the woman had donated to see if any of it would fill gaps in our collection. When I thought I had seen everything and was going to discard the bags the donor had brought the items in, I realized that one of the bags seemed to be a little heavier than the other two. That one also had a lot of water stains on it. I felt around inside the bag and found that there was another bag at the bottom! I pulled out the compressed paper bag and opened it very carefully. Inside were two clothing items of silk crepe. The items were badly stained from the water that they must have absorbed long ago in the damp cellar. I took them out and gently laid them on the examination table. They were both very crumpled.

While carefully examining them, I found that one item was a sleeveless dress and the other a long-sleeved matching jacket of the same fabric and color. Both items had been beautifully hand sewn with matching silk thread. They appeared to be in fair condition except for being heavily compressed. The trim had lots of pleats that had suffered greatly from the water, and the original color, which had probably been a mint green shade had faded.

While examining this garment, I looked inside to see if there was a label. There was a label, and it was a designer label! I was very excited when I discovered it, for I knew who the French fashion designer was, and I knew of her work. She was quite famous in the 1930–40 period, and we did not have any of her designs in our collection. I was very happy, for this designer original would certainly be a noteworthy and welcome addition to the collection.

The following weeks, I devoted some time to restoring the two-piece fashion, and eventually it was in good enough condition to be safely exhibited. Unfortunately, because there was no record of who wore it or when or why or even where it came from, there was nothing to add to the file. I satisfied myself by realizing that the label had given some valuable information; it would be a start for someone wanting to research the designer and her work. However, I wished there was also something to tell us about the original owner. I imagined that whoever she was, she most certainly at one time in the past must have really enjoyed wearing her very lovely designer original.

I find that when people find old clothes packed away with no information or any interest in how the items are stored, such situations like the one just mentioned happen. Sometimes when we think about textile objects in our homes, we are more likely to be aware of what is on display rather than what might be stored away. For example, we may treat old wall hangings and other interior furnishings made of textiles with special care because we are familiar with them and feel that they are of some value. They may be heirloom articles handed down through the years, and because they belonged to one's ancestors, they continue to be treated as precious remembrances and handled carefully by each succeeding generation.

Antique clothing items, however, are not usually displayed in a home but are packed away in trunks, closets, cellars, or an attic. The garments were put away by someone to hopefully be unpacked later on for some other occasion, with no one really thinking that they might be damaged by their time in storage. Often items are tucked away in an out-of-the-way location and totally forgotten about by the family, and when their house is getting ready to be sold, the items surface. If a family has lived for many generations in a house, the clothing in storage may also turn out to be rare and of historic value.

Unless an old garment is a wedding gown, christening dress, or some other memorable garment with carefully recorded history, future family members might not even know it exists. When discovering such an object, they may not think it of value and just leave it where it is or toss it out.

Mistakes can be made when one has no idea of why something was saved and, not knowing, just assumes it is nothing important. Whether it is saved because of special family history, unique beauty, or perceived value is not the issue. What matters now is the way in which it is to be stored, if one is hoping to keep it safe for any future use.

Wedding gowns and other textile objects are frequently put away in a hurry and not stored correctly. They may be damaged if they were not packed carefully initially and may continue to deteriorate greatly over the years. In much earlier times, most everything that was put away in storage was carefully placed in large, heavy trunks, well wrapped and protected in their secure mini-environment.

The trunks were well built and pretty airtight, keeping out dampness, insects, and vermin. Consequently, the garments, textiles, and other items inside were all pretty thoroughly protected. Unfortunately, many years later the trunk might be opened and the objects removed and handled improperly by a curious individual. Very often, finding an old dress or other treasure is an exciting experience, and the first impulse for the discoverer is to want to try it on. More often than not, when that happens, one does not think to note the age or fragility of the garment. Nor does one consider, when wanting to wear it, if it is vintage or very old. One might not know about special period foundations or undergarments that would have been worn with it to give the proper silhouette and support. Plus, if one decides to try on any of the garments in the trunk and is not careful, the seams may split, the fabric shred, and any of the resulting damage to the items might be irreversible.

Figure 19. Four-poster bed, trunk, and quilt, nineteenth century.

Needless to say, I believe that one needs to consider all of this if one discovers a trunk full of such items, and use caution. Remember that when packing clothing and other objects, one should always try to help protect them from damage. Unless an old garment is a wedding gown or a family christening dress or some other item with some carefully recorded history, family members might just not think to store it with great care, especially if they do not know how to store such items properly.

When I decide to put items in storage, I usually take a photograph of the garment or other object from different angles, putting it on a padded hanger or dress form when available. I find that this method is especially helpful because the photo will often show the object at its best. It can also help to protect the object for future generations by helping to limit the amount of handling. Later on, one can first view the photo and then decide if one really needs to disturb the actual garment.

Also, I like to remind others that written descriptions and interesting provenance to accompany the photos are good to have, because people do forget. Such written or recorded information can become valuable for additional research and be a source for study concerning the history of the garment, if more is wanted years in the future.

I always put the information on the outside of the storage container (preferably an acid-free box with acid-free tissue used to wrap items) whenever storing a carefully padded and tissue-wrapped garment or other object. I find it is important, for it not only serves to identify the object but keeps it from being disturbed if it is not what one might think is in the container. If information is placed on a container, I also put the same information inside, safely attached to the container so that it cannot get dislodged if the container is moved. If a garment is to be hung (see information discussed in a previous chapter regarding hangers) rather than boxed, I also like to have a label or special tag attached to the outside protective covering placed over the garment being hung, with necessary information and photos. This prevents the garment from having to be disturbed unnecessarily. I always remember to be careful when recording information for vintage and older garments and other textile objects if they are stored this way. I try to keep the information neat and concise and like to use small copies of photos attached to the labels whenever possible and make sure there are no sharp edges on any of the labels or photos that could damage the objects.

Now, I have written a brief moment to share with you, to give you an example of a garment that might be a candidate for storage:

It was a beautiful day ...

She is walking down the aisle, a vision of beauty in her gown of pure white. The music is filling the room, seeming to embrace the shimmering satin and pristine layers of handmade lace that rustle with each step she takes. The procession has begun, and the bride and her gown are in their full glory, a dream come true ...

From this moment on, however, we find that the aging process has begun, with potential damage to this ceremonial garment. The bride's bouquet, her nervous perspiration, and any soil from the church floor and the carpeting covering the floor can all contribute to the moment, as well as the more obvious makeup, hairspray, and perfume.

During the reception, the bride and her gown will come in contact with many hugs, kisses, food, and beverages. Once the festivities reach the point where the happy and now married couple changes into their honeymoon "going-away clothes," the wedding gown and accessories have a brief moment before they are put away.

What happens to these cherished articles next determines whether they remain in good condition for the future and a next possible appearance or become a problem and disappointment that someone else may have to deal with. Whenever we decide to protect our treasures for the future, of course we want to do the best we can, so that when we or someone else retrieve that item later on, all the information and the object will be safe and available.

If a gown is soiled after being worn, it most likely needs to be cleaned before storage. Today there are a number of people and companies that will, for a fee, not only clean a wedding gown for a customer but also provide special storage containers. Because gowns of this type often are quite elaborate, people sometimes obtain this type of special packaging, especially if they plan on keeping their gown for someone to wear in the future.

When planning to store items for the future, remember to be sure they are clean and properly padded and wrapped, with pertinent information on the container. One may want to periodically check on their location, just to make sure that the storage area and any special containers have not been disturbed.

Please feel free to refer to our conversations in this book when you are looking for ideas or suggestions on the subject matter. These are only examples for you to ponder when making your own decisions. Remember that any you make are of course yours alone. It is all a matter of choice. I sincerely hope that reading this book has given you a better understanding of the nature and needs of aged clothing, textiles, and related objects.

Summary

When I was almost finished writing this book, I thought it might also be helpful to the reader if I went back and touched on the many topics we have discussed briefly, to provide an overview or summary of the basic contents of this book. Therefore, I have written a short description of each chapter, taking them in order and making some general comments that relate to the particular subject matter. It is hoped that this will be helpful and a handy reference for you to refer back to if you should so desire in the future. As you have discovered by reading this book, each chapter begins with a story that leads into what will be discussed.

We will begin now with a basic summary of chapter 1, entitled "Closets." My grandmother's closet was used to set the stage for our adventure and introduce you to the process of discovery. Sometimes interesting aged articles surface unexpectedly in ordinary places. They may not be the least bit familiar to us when we see them for the first time, and as a result, we may not have any idea of what it is we have found. However, if we are curious about our discoveries or think they may have some value, we often have questions, and then we may be tempted to find ways to learn more about them.

When coming across antique or vintage clothing items in particular, we may find ourselves wondering how they looked on a person long ago. Asking questions is a good way to start the research process. Remember the conversations I had with my grandmother. It was while visiting with her that I became excited, discovering that her bedroom closet held some very interesting items I had never seen before. I had lots of questions for her. In the story, I relay some of the discussions we had and what my grandmother said to me about restrictive items she wore during early periods in her life, to share with you some of what life was like for women then.

Some historic items are mentioned in detail. I talk about clothing and what was required to keep one's figure, along with some types of restrictive underpinnings that would have been needed when wearing a fashionable period garment. Of course, how it looked on a person might not just relate to a body covering, such as a corset, but might include other types of clothing accessories as well. We explore the subject matter a bit further.

Investigating other ways of finding clues is discussed, and the process is continued when I tell you about my time spent in an old attic in an early historic house where a particularly important aged garment surfaced. I discuss the experience and some of the procedures and cautions one may want to consider when working in such a setting with fragile historic objects.

Chapter 2, entitled "Different Times," begins with memories. In this chapter, we discuss family and their treasures and stories so often left behind for others to unravel. I wanted to share my experiences with you regarding discovery because how one handles their newly found or recently inherited antique textiles and clothing is important.

Here I walk you through a little bit more of the process to help you think about what you will want to do when coming upon these treasures and why careful handling is particularly important when dealing with old, fragile items. A few of the procedures are described in detail for one to think about when handling newly discovered antique garments and other aged objects, for those of you who find or inherit a trunk full of items in the attic. I also give additional information and clues that might help one to recognize and date period clothing and accessories.

Chapter 3 I named "Fashion Snippets" to carry the discovery process even further and talk a little more about what people from our past experienced and why clothing and other articles from their time were so important to them. Knowing how much emphasis was placed on textile and clothing by the early settlers in America helps us understand and appreciate a little more about their customs and what their lives were like. Here I provide information on some of the skills they had to help them produce goods they needed.

Also included is more historical information, and I talk about how our country progressed in the field of textiles in more detail, starting with early production and advancing forward to some interesting developments that occurred over the years.

Clothing was not the only product of the time worth appreciating, and we examine other textile items in chapter 4, which I entitled "Bits and Pieces." Lots of people today love old textiles, whether they are handwoven coverlets or other kinds of household goods, including hand-sewn quilts made from printed and plain fabrics and accessories, such as assorted wraps and other flat textiles. Here I delve into history in a little more detail and discuss some of these early textile items so popular at the time.

I take you to a quilting bee in this chapter, too, and explain some of the early customs and interests that are a part of our history where small bits and larger pieces of textiles played interesting roles. Because there are many beautiful, hand-sewn quilts still surviving that were created for homes many years ago, I describe a number of the different types of quilts, including pieced quilts, whole cloth quilts, and other bed covers. I describe how they were made and some patterns and techniques used to identify and date them.

Chapter 5 takes us a little further into textiles made from natural fibers. I chose the title "All Natural" because in this chapter we become more involved in the actual composition of textiles and talk about various natural fibers, fabrics made from them, and their characteristics.

I discuss in detail fiber production, hand weaving, and manufacture of the early textile fabrics, and I comment on a few specific textile items. This is done to help provide more information on early textile products and includes those that were produced at home in the early days, to explain how textile manufacturing has changed over time, in order that one might be able to find clues to help one date them more easily.

I also discuss how we have gone from producing natural fiber fabrics to man-made fabrics and finishes and then to some extent how history seems to be repeating itself.

Chapter 6 is entitled "Summer Heat" and begins with a story about how not to care for an antique fan. There are many collectors who love their antiques. Some may also attempt to display them at home, and one may occasionally even see someone wearing a vintage garment at a party or carrying an accessory made from an attractive aged textile or related object. We enjoy our treasures. Some of us realize that they are fragile and want to know how to care for them, and others may not particularly think to worry about care. What can happen to the treasure we are so fond of depends on the condition of the object and whether or not we know how to handle it properly.

There are particular signs of deterioration to look for when examining aged textiles, and I explain what they may look like and provide some suggestions for care and handling in detail. When one understands a few basic principles and is more aware of fragility and proper handling considerations, one can feel more secure with aged textiles and similar items. Because people might want to use their textile items in many different ways, I also provide examples of some ways I display aged objects. I explain why using common sense and various techniques might help when working on a costume exhibit.

Chapter 7 is based on the many questions that came to me in my work as a curator dealing with the care of aged textiles and clothing items. I entitled it "Oh No!" to emphasize the need to pay attention.

Here I discuss the fragility of aged textiles and how to recognize potential problems before an "Oh no!" might happen. I talk about ways to recognize and understand aged textiles and why we need to be made aware of the dangers that can occur with improper handling.

I also discuss why it is important to use common sense and gather helpful information before making decisions.

There are often lots of questions regarding cleaning old garments and such, and so I felt it would be good if I described a wet cleaning method I use, along with some other treatments I implement when caring for aged textile items. None of this is meant to be taken as definite advice; I provide only an explanation of how I have performed the processes myself, so one can have the opportunity to think through carefully what was involved and gain a better understanding of why I proceeded the way I did in the examples I have given. There is much to think about when treating aged textiles, and one should always proceed with caution. I have merely written all this to serve as a guide.

Chapter 8 I called "The Shawl and the Piano." An unusual title until you read the story. This chapter is fairly specific and geared mostly toward antique dealers and other shop owners who want to have information relating to how one may properly prepare and display items for sale. I explain that there are a number of things that one might want to consider, including an awareness of value, being knowledgeable enough to understand how to handle aged textile objects on display that are for sale, condition issues that might need to be dealt with, and how to present the information correctly. Later on, we see that small museums and other such facilities have similar concerns, but of course their needs have more to do with long-term ownership.

Chapter 9 is named "Arms and Legs." It too has a rather interesting title, and I think explains itself quite well. Here I expand on the last chapter and get into more detail. Displaying aged garments can be done in many ways, but dressing mannequins in aged garments can be very tricky if one does not understand aged textiles. How to dress them safely with actual aged garments can be time consuming, but being careful is important and takes practice.

There have been many different types of mannequins over the years, and today there are quite a few new and innovative forms on display in department stores and large museums. Some are quite costly, however, and not all small museums, shops, and other such facilities have the funds to invest in new ones and have to work only with what is affordable.

I discuss how to use such equipment in much detail and what types of situations might require caution and even some ingenuity. I discuss how one needs to consider the textile and remember that how it is handled is of primary concern in the process. We also discuss some different techniques for displaying textiles in antique shops, small museums, and historical society facilities.

Chapter 10 is entitled "Lessons to Learn," and the beginning story starts out with an example of what happened when a small historical society had an exhibit done by an individual who didn't do enough research on the historic objects to be displayed before setting it up. Here I explain why it is really important to have some training, along with thorough knowledge of fashions to be exhibited and the collections one works with.

I go into great detail discussing different types of historic collections and the various types of buildings used for small museums, local historical societies, and other such facilities where historic items are housed. I also talk about the importance of recognizing the need for staff and their volunteers to have proper training and a good understanding of their collections. This includes the need for in-depth training involving documentation, care, display, and storage of collections.

I give a lot of information and examples of methods I have used and certain particulars that I believe might be helpful and encouraging to those who are thinking of finding more efficient ways to operate their costume collections. Here I talk about my own work experiences and get into details regarding collection management, particular inventory methods, and care for aged costume and textiles. My focus here is to share some of my own actions and experiences and procedures I used to improve the collection facility I managed, so that it might generate a few ideas that could perhaps be of some help to other small collection facilities in similar situations.

I named chapter 11 "Show Biz." This chapter was fun to write, and I hope it is helpful especially for semiprofessional theater companies, reenactment groups, and academic institutions with theater classes that might have small collections of aged textiles and clothing items. I wrote this to help them be aware of some methods that might help them learn how to properly use or wear theater costumes or study pieces that are aged garments and also protect them from damage.

In the opening story, I talk about one of the times that I was involved in working with costume and wardrobe people in a major film. Here we can see how those costumes were used and how some costumes for the stage and film are used differently from those that are housed in a museum. If any of the pieces they have are to be used for a costume, one is either wearing the object onstage or using the aged garment as a pattern to construct a stage costume. I talk about ways to use such clothing and textile items that may be part of a theater wardrobe and also discuss safety measures in the wearing and storing of aged garments that are valued costume pieces.

Using an antique garment to create a costume and keeping the original for research is discussed. If the original is to be worn onstage, proper handling is important to consider, and I provide some information on different periods and what to look for when modeling these garments. Different periods have different characteristics that need to be recognized when one is working with an antique garment or accessory. How a costume piece is handled depends on the different types of fabrics it contains, the construction and condition of the garment, and how it looks on the actor.

Chapter 12 is the last one and is called "Treasures Found." Here I continue with the story, and then we "go home" and summarize our experiences. I also provide extra information at the end on how to place and protect treasures in storage. After all, sometimes we just don't know what to do with old clothing and other aged items and find that we want to save them in case they might come in handy later on.

For example, a wedding gown is a garment one may not want to discard because it is beautiful, and someday perhaps another family member or relative will want to wear it. It certainly is the type of garment where memories can take center stage, and because of that, one might decide to keep it.

Whenever we want to keep special items and start thinking about packing them away for the future, of course we have decisions to make, and in this chapter I make note of the type of steps I might consider before deciding how to continue. And then, when the decisions have been made and implemented, one can "close the trunk," hopefully protecting the treasures for their next appearances.

And now, when thinking about all of what we have talked about, I know that a lot of the subject matter is gleaned from my many and varied experiences as a curator and other related positions I have had up to now, but I do believe a lot of it also relates to using a commonsense approach in one's thinking. I sincerely hope that my conversations on the topics discussed have helped you think about aged textiles in a whole new way, that they have been informative, and that you have enjoyed the journey!

Postscript

We have talked about closets used to store clothes, shoes, and hats.
Room for other memories, there is no doubt about that.
We find trunks in an attic, laden with stories to be told.
And sometimes what we find seems worth more than gold.
They yearn to be cherished, for they carry vibrations.
And some will go on for many generations.

—Alda G. Kaye

CPSIA information can be obtained
at www.ICGtesting.com
Printed in the USA
FFOW05n1528171115